America
on my mind

Introduction by
Jimmy Carter

FALCON PRESS®

From the Publisher,

We have worked for more than three years to bring you *America on My Mind.* During that time, it has become more than a book; it has become a reminder of all that is good and right about our nation. The words and photographs are testaments to that. But even more important, this book has given us hope for the future of America—a future that lies pliable in the hands of its children.

Featured in this book are the prose and poetry of 100 school children from throughout the country. These works are the best of about 18,000 entries in a national writing contest sponsored by the Young Writer's Contest Foundation. The entries illustrate the love and hope these youngsters have for their country, as well as the talent with which they will shape its future.

Illiteracy is growing at an alarming rate. But the writings in this book are proof that illiteracy can be overcome if we continue our commitment to the fight. In keeping with that sentiment, we have donated a portion of the proceeds from the sale of this book to Ronald McDonald Children's Charities. RMCC, in turn, will use the money to help promote literacy and to further its other charitable works, such as the Ronald McDonald Houses. We and RMCC also have donated another $30,000 to the schools that the winners of the Young Writer's Contest attend. The schools will use the money to buy much-needed reading materials.

Former President Jimmy Carter, Ronald McDonald Children's Charities, and the Young Writer's Contest Foundation have joined us in a special partnership to celebrate our country and our hopes for its future. Through *America on My Mind,* we also express our united concern for the future if illiteracy continues to increase.

We wish to thank our partners for their support. Without their help, this book would not have been possible. We also wish to thank the young writers for their participation and to salute them for their desire to learn and to keep America strong and beautiful. *America on My Mind* is dedicated to them.

FALCON PRESS®

*Falcon Press Publishing Co.
Helena and Billings, Montana*

Moonrise over the Lower Falls of the Yellowstone River, Yellowstone National Park, Wyoming   GREG L. RYAN / SALLY A. BEYER

Yellow irises adding color to Red House Lake, Allegheny State Park, New York   CARR CLIFTON

Upper Yosemite Falls plunging 1,430 feet into Yosemite Valley, Yosemite National Park, California DAVID MUENCH

the beauty and promise of America

I grew up as a farm boy three miles west of Plains, Georgia, where one of the 650 residents was my future wife, Rosalynn. During those depression years, our house did not have electricity or running water, and our Southern society was plagued by almost total racial segregation. One exception was that black and white farm families labored long and hard in the fields, side by side. The financial rewards were minimal, but even then—from our patriotic church sermons, history lessons, and school debates on issues of national interest—we knew the beauty and promise of America.

After decades of soil erosion caused by repetitive cotton crops, my father was building terraces, protecting wildlife habitat, planting trees, and practicing contour farming. We worked hard, but we also learned to enjoy and respect the great gifts of the land. After the crops were ''laid by,'' or after a rain when it was too wet to plow, we children spent our free time in the woods and swamps—exploring, hunting, and fishing. We learned where the seasonal fruits, nuts, and berries grew, the need to control soil erosion and to protect wildlife habitat. The squirrels, rabbits, opossums, raccoons, catfish, and eels we caught were a proud contribution to our families' tables.

Education was a top priority in my family. There was a remarkable teacher in our small school who enticed me to read endless lists of literary classics. He made all of us white kids memorize the names of famous artists and their works and listen repeatedly to scratchy recordings of some of the world's greatest music. I am reluctant to admit that in those early days I gave little thought to how my black playmates were being educated in their segregated school. ''Separate but equal'' was a totally inaccurate but soporific phrase.

As an adult, I can understand at least partially how our resilient and self-correcting society could have allowed one of us to occupy the nation's highest political office and all of us to remove the millstone of racism from our necks. I know that as a Georgian I could not have been considered seriously as a presidential candidate if the South still had been suffering from this tragic heritage. The pioneer American spirit still blesses us with the ability to respond to personal opportunities and to correct our nation's faults.

No one could visit all fifty states, as I have, without being inspired by the beauty and grandeur of our land and seas, our prairies and mountains, our forests and deserts. Some of the vistas seem common-place; others are truly breathtaking. There are stark differences among the Okefenokee Swamp, the cityscape of San Francisco, the red fields of Georgia, and the Brooks Range of Alaska. Most extraordinary of all are the people. No other nation has such a diverse population. Many families still have ties to relatives in foreign countries and venerate their Old-World language, history, religion, music, and culture. At the same time, we are drawn together by one common force: a commitment to freedom.

Our country has its share of problems, including poverty, illiteracy, and

Fly fishing for trout on the Madison River, Yellowstone National Park, Montana / Wyoming / Idaho   MICHAEL S. SAMPLE

homelessness. Some of our natural treasures are being despoiled by greed and the misplaced priorities of economic "progress." But we are able to face these challenges with the same drive of the pioneer days, a drive based on determination, courage, hard work, and new ideas.

We are, indeed, still a pioneer nation. Cherishing our precious natural sites exemplifies this heritage. We like to explore, to face the unexpected, and to see the world as God made it. I know how deeply and beneficially my own life is affected by experiences in wild areas. My family still enjoys adventures all the way from Georgia's Okefenokee Swamp to the mountain peaks and glaciers of the Northwest. We fish the warm waters of Georgia and Florida, but we also relish our annual excursions to the trout streams of Pennsylvania, Colorado, Montana, Washington, Oregon, and Alaska. It is to our nation's credit that we protect these outdoor treasures. But tragically, not all Americans share these values. The environmental struggle goes on. Recently, in the Alaska Wildlife Refuge, we were able to access this confrontation.

From a high plateau in the Brooks Range, we observed a flock of three dozen mountain sheep moving delicately above us, feeding on the sparse lichens. Later, we stood quietly as a sea of caribou split and streamed by us on both sides. Just a few yards from the Beaufort Sea, we watched a family of vigilant musk oxen graze, while guarding their frolicking

calves. There are few places on earth that are so unspoiled, so beautiful, so filled with wildlife, so fragile. All this is endangered by shortsighted leaders who would permanently despoil this vast area with drilling rigs and pumping stations, attempting to assuage our extravagant thirst for oil for just a few additional months.

A continuing embarrassment, even after the civil rights victories, is the disinclination or inability of our rich country to alleviate the suffering of our fellow citizens. Homelessness is pervasive. Fifty thousand of our neighbors in New York City will have no shelter tonight, and several million other Americans across our country share this tragedy. Although serious, this is not an insoluble problem.

Rosalynn and I have lived in a governor's mansion and in the White House and have visited with kings and presidents in their palaces. But the most wonderful dwellings we know are the modest homes being built with eager hands by volunteers and some of America's poorest families—working side by side as equals. "The only two good things in our old house was me and my husband," said one proud woman in Philadelphia. Other new homeowners, who have never had a high school diploma to frame for the wall, almost immediately begin to pick out colleges for their children. This spirit of caring and sharing has been one of the great strengths of our country—people with confidence in the future, working together for a better life.

Illiteracy is also a serious infliction. The value of reading and writing is made clear by the poems and essays in this book by the Young Writer's Contest winners, supported by Ronald McDonald Children's Charities. But almost one-third of our adult citizens are unable to read them. I have helped to educate parents who could not

Proud artist in kindergarten, Cambridge, Massachusetts FRANK SITEMAN / NE STOCK PHOTO

fill out a job application, tell what street they were on, or know what items were on a menu. Their plight is almost incomprehensible to those of us who are literate. With modern electronic teaching aids and with a national commitment to literacy, this failure can be corrected. Other countries, not so strong and innovative as ours, have done so.

Strength and real patriotism require a frank assessment of both our achievements and our disappointments. A society can be judged by its ability to set high standards of truth, justice, beauty, and peace and by its willingness to alleviate human suffering, acknowledge its faults, and face challenges successfully. America is truly blessed and beautiful—both with its natural resources and with its people—but we cannot afford to be satisfied or complacent. Meeting the obligation to preserve our treasures and to build even better lives is the measure of our nation's greatness.

Jimmy Carter

Jimmy Carter

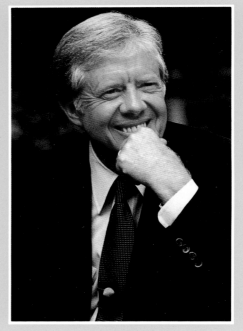

Jimmy Carter

Toccoa Falls, scenic attraction on the campus of Toccoa Falls College in northeast Georgia   ED COOPER

Young Writer's Contest Grand Prize Winner for America on My Mind

Patriotism

Patriotism—love for our country and an unending
     devotion to it—is the good and right
     thing that binds America together.
Images of patriotism flash before our eyes like
     lightning daily.

The sun gleaming through majestic American flags
     as they gallantly snap and sway over
     green grass and gray tombstones in a
     national cemetery on Veteran's Day.
People hanging over highway overpasses yelling
     and whooping words of encouragement
     to young soldiers on their way to a
     world a million miles away.
American Olympic gold medal winners' voices
     breaking and eyes glistening as they hail
     their flag and sing their national anthem
     in front of the world.
The soldiers at Iwo Jima, though exhausted,
     raising their flag as artillery rings in their
     ears, smoke stings their nostrils, and
     blasts of fire fill the air.
Veterans, some upright, some handicapped, some
     slumped in wheelchairs, saluting the
     strains of ''The Star Spangled Banner'' as
     they float through the still air.
Baseball players, dressed in their unsoiled whites,
     their cleats resting on the vivid green
     grass, removing their caps and placing
     them over their hearts as the singer and
     the organist key up to salute their
     country.
The stark blackness of the Vietnam Veterans
     Memorial matching the mournful
     countenance of the respectful people
     who file past the infinite sandblasted
     names.
Flags plastered on rustic country mailboxes and
     red, white, and blue streamers fluttering
     like doves on car radio antennas in
     honor of the U.S. servicemen in the
     Middle East.

P
  a
    t
      r
        i
          o
            t
          i
            s
              m

is America at its best.
May it always remain that way.

Jeffrey Fallis, Grade 8
Teacher: Margaret Wingate
Pine Mountain Middle School
Kennesaw, Georgia

Portrait of an adult bald eagle on the Nisqually River, Washington
TOM & PAT LEESON

Two-thousand-year-old giant sequoias resplendent in snow at Sequoia National Park, California   DAVID MUENCH

Approaching the American Falls portion of Niagara Falls, New York
SAM ABELL

Autumn in White River National Forest, Colorado
JEFF GNASS

Other nations have glorious mountains, breath-taking views. But none can approach the incomparable variety of wild beauty that is the heritage of this land—with its Yosemite, its Niagara, its Grand Canyon, its Old Faithful, its Carlsbad Caverns, its timberline gardens and deserts bursting into bloom, its Olympic forests and its ancient sequoias, its snow-clad peaks and all the teeming bird life of its coastal swamps. This gift of natural beauty is a rare and precious possession. The opportunity for citizens to enjoy it freely, now and in the future, is one of the inalienable rights of Americans.

Edwin Way Teale,
Journey into Summer

Redbud blossoms adding color to a spring morning at Kelly's Ford, Virginia   SAM ABELL

Cedar waxwing with apple blossoms near Madison, Wisconsin   WAYNE LANKINEN / DRK PHOTO

" America my country,
A nation proud and free,
From the mountains to the
valleys,
How beautiful to me. "

Matthew Gorski, Grade 5,
Hampstead, New Hampshire.
From ''America My Country''
in the Young Writer's Contest.

Autumn splendor in Great Smoky Mountains National Park, Tennessee / North Carolina LARRY ULRICH

Maple-lined country road near Woodstock, Vermont STEVE TERRILL

Sunrise over a sea of clouds in the Cascade Mountains, Washington CLIFF LEIGHT

Something happened in America to create the Americans. Perhaps it was the grandeur of the land—the lordly mountains, the mystery of deserts, the ache of storms, cyclones—the enormous sweetness and violence of the country which, acting on restless, driven people from the outside world, made them taller than their ancestors, stronger than their fathers—and made them all Americans.

John Steinbeck,
America and Americans

Mark Allen of Cardiff, California, winning the 1989 Ironman Triathlon in record time (8:09:15), Kona, Hawaii   GREG VAUGHN

Blueberry leaves celebrating autumn on Mount Desert Island, Acadia National Park, Maine LARRY ULRICH

Quiet morning amid the boats and lobster pots of Corea, Maine   WILLARD CLAY

Black ducks in a red dawn, Blackwater National Wildlife Refuge, Chesapeake Bay,
Maryland   SCOTT NIELSEN

Hoodoos—fluted columns of limestone and sandstone—in Bryce Canyon National Park, Utah   FRED HIRSCHMANN

" In the United States there is more space where nobody is than where everybody is. That is what makes America what it is. "

Gertrude Stein,
The Geographical History of America

Forty-foot-tall Joshua trees silhouetted by sunset at Joshua Tree National Monument, California   WILLARD CLAY

White wolf on the prowl in northern Minnesota   DANIEL J. COX

" *Silently as a feather falls to the earth,*
It runs through the woods
With the speed of the wind
And the beauty of the dawn. . . .
It is a living legend,
The wolf. "

Julia Price, Grade 6,
Rexburg, Idaho.
From ''The Wolf'' in the
Young Writer's Contest.

Moonrise over 20,320-foot Mount McKinley, highest peak in America, Denali National Park, Alaska   TOM J. ULRICH

Presidents Washington, Jefferson, Roosevelt, and Lincoln created equally and permanently at Mount Rushmore, South Dakota   AIUPPY PHOTOGRAPHS

We hold these truths to be self-evident, that all men are created equal, that they are endowed by their Creator with certain unalienable Rights, that among these are Life, Liberty and the pursuit of Happiness.

Thomas Jefferson,
Declaration of Independence

The Mormon Tabernacle Choir arrayed for song, Salt Lake City, Utah   STEPHEN TRIMBLE

Hutterite girls pulling together near Forest River, North Dakota   ANNIE GRIFFITHS BELT

Pursuing happiness with Mickey at Disneyland, California   JAMES KIRK GARDNER

Sunrise coming to the fog-cloaked Ouachita Mountains in west-central Arkansas   MATT BRADLEY

Monarch butterfly on a marigold, Decorah, Iowa
DAVID CAVAGNARO/DRK PHOTO

Blackfeet tipis at Browning, Montana   CHRIS ROBERTS

Shoshone-Bannock warrior in traditional dress, Shoshone, Idaho   DAVID STOECKLEIN

❝ *So that they will respect the land, tell your children that the earth is rich with the lives of our kin. Teach your children what we have taught our children, that the earth is our mother. Whatever befalls the earth befalls the sons of the earth. Man did not weave the web of life, he is merely a strand in it. Whatever he does to the web, he does to himself.* **❞**

Chief Seattle,
to President Franklin Pierce

Autumn-colored foothills of the San Juan Range, Uncompahgre National Forest, Colorado   WILLARD CLAY

Linton Spring plunging through the 242,400-acre Three Sisters Wilderness, Willamette National Forest, Oregon   LARRY ULRICH

Navigating Fish Creek, a tributary of the Lochsa River
near Cougar, Idaho   SCOTT SPIKER

Hiking the Bachelor Meadows Trail in Glacier National Park,
Montana   PETER COLE / NE STOCK PHOTO

31

Kayaking on Swiftcurrent Lake, Glacier National Park, Montana   JAMES RANDKLEV

Siblings sharing the catch at Otter Creek Reservoir, Utah
JAMES KIRK GARDNER

Wildflowers—Indian paintbrush, lupines, and alpine daisies—at Mount Rainier National Park, Washington   ART WOLFE

Paying homage at Lincoln's Tomb,
Springfield, Illinois   RICHARD HAMILTON SMITH

Indian girl at Taos Pueblo Intertribal
Pow Wow, New Mexico   KEN GALLARD

*“ Our flag is red, white, and blue, but our nation
is a rainbow—red, yellow, brown, black, and white—and
we're all precious in God's sight. America is not like a
blanket—one piece of unbroken cloth, the same color, the same
texture, the same size. America is more like a quilt—many
patches, many pieces, many colors, many sizes, all woven and
held together by a common thread.... All of us count and all
of us fit somewhere. ”*

Jesse Jackson,
speech before the
Democratic National Convention,
July 16, 1984

Naturalization ceremony with Russian ballet dancer Mikhail Baryshnikov, New York City   ANNIE GRIFFITHS BELT / DRK PHOTO

Chef in Washington, D.C.   CATHERINE KARNOW

Logger in northwestern Montana   LEE KAISER

Canoeing the Buffalo National River, Arkansas   MATT BRADLEY

Raccoon at home in northern Georgia   DANIEL J. COX

> **❝** . . . *the peculiar history of the South has so greatly modified it from the general American norm that, when viewed as a whole, it decisively justifies the notion that the country is—not quite a nation within a nation, but the next thing to it.* **❞**

W. J. Cash,
The Mind of the South

Analyzing the day's events at the Gilbert General Store, Gilbert, Arkansas   MATT BRADLEY

Tempting trout at Pigeon Forge Mill in eastern Tennessee
GREG L. RYAN / SALLY A. BEYER

Quilter at Madison, Mississippi
J. D. SCHWALM / STOCK SOUTH

Space shuttle *Discovery* lifting off at Cape Canaveral, Florida
ALLEN FREDRICKSON / THIRD COAST STOCK SOURCE

Celebrating the summit of 9,415-foot Mount Stuart in the Central Cascades, Wenatchee National Forest, Washington   CLIFF LEIGHT

“ *Nothing so challenges the American spirit as tackling the biggest job on earth.... Americans are stimulated by the big job—the Panama Canal, ...the tallest building in the world, the mightiest battleship.* ”

Lyndon B. Johnson,
speech to Congress,
April 30, 1941

Golden Gate Bridge in morning fog, San Francisco, California CATHERINE KARNOW

Space Needle piercing the skyline of Seattle, Washington SCOTT SPIKER

The twin-spired Sears Tower, tallest building in the world, rising above massive skyscrapers in downtown Chicago, Illinois TERRY FARMER / PHOTOGRAPHIC RESOURCES

Highway 163 heading across the desert to Monument Valley, Arizona   TOM BEAN / DRK PHOTO

❝ One of the special pleasures about a back road in the West is that it sometimes ends dead against a wonderful and relatively unvisited wilderness. ❞

Wallace Stegner,
''Packhorse Paradise,'' in
The Sound of Mountain Water

Water-sculpted canyon on the Colorado Plateau, Utah   FRED HIRSCHMANN

Greeting the sun at Toroweap Point, far above the Colorado River in Grand Canyon National Park, Arizona   RANDALL K. ROBERTS

Evening light on the Vista House visitor center in the Columbia River Gorge National Scenic Area, Oregon   STEVE TERRILL

> *This is a glorious country. It has longer rivers and more of them, and they are muddier and deeper and run faster, and rise higher, and make more noise and fall lower... than anybody else's rivers. It has more lakes and they are bigger and deeper and clearer and wetter than those of any other country.*

American newspaper,
1850

Sailboarding in the Columbia River Gorge, Washington / Oregon
SCOTT SPIKER

The rushing waters of the Carbon River in western Washington PAT O'HARA

Starfish and kelp waiting for the tide to turn at Devil's Punchbowl State Park, Oregon   DENNIS HENRY

The shore has a dual nature, changing with the swing of the tides, belonging now to the land, now to the sea. On the ebb tide it knows the harsh extremes of the land world, being exposed to heat and cold, to wind, to rain and drying sun. On the flood tide it is a water world, returning briefly to the relative stability of the open sea.

Rachel Carson,
The Edge of the Sea

Sunset on the rocky shores of Rialto Beach, Olympic National Park, Washington   CARR CLIFTON

Digging for clams near Long Beach, Washington   STEVE MASON / DRS PRODUCTIONS

Portland Head Light marking a rocky point of Casco Bay, Portland, Maine   LARRY ULRICH

Horned puffins on parade, Pribilof Islands, Alaska
STEPHEN J. KRASEMANN / DRK PHOTO

Na Pali Cliffs falling away about 2,000 feet to the Pacific on Kauai, Hawaii   FRANS LANTING / MINDEN PICTURES

Sunrise illuminating a ghostly grove of cypress stumps in Atchafalaya Swamp, Louisiana   EASTCOTT / MOMATIUK / DRK PHOTO

Waiting for the sea to swallow the sun, Daufuskie Island, South Carolina ANNIE GRIFFITHS BELT

End of the day at Naples, Florida MICHAEL S. SAMPLE

Knowledge is a mighty thing
To have in the hand,
But I would trade it all
If I could only understand.

Karen Paik, Grade 8,
Burlingame, California.
From "Understanding" in the
Young Writer's Contest.

Autumn along the Hudson River near Bear Mountain State Park, New York   CARR CLIFTON

Staghorn sumac leaves   S. NIELSEN

Pine grosbeak   JOHN GERLACH / DRK PHOTO

Maple leaves   DOUGLAS MERRIAM

“ Autumn is the American season. In Europe the leaves turn yellow or brown, and fall. Here they take fire on the trees and hang there flaming. We think this frost-fire is a portent somehow: a promise that the continent has given us. Life, too, we think, is capable of taking fire in this country. ”

Archibald MacLeish,
"Sweet Land of Liberty" Collier's,
July 8, 1955

October colors at East Orange, Vermont   JEFF GNASS

Upper Falls of the Tahquamenon River in Tahquamenon Falls State Park, northern Michigan   DAVID MUENCH

Autumn yielding to winter on the White Mountains in New Hampshire   STEPHEN TRIMBLE

Little Red Wagon Sidewalk Sweeping Service in
Moscow, Idaho   SCOTT SPIKER

Dawn over the Appalachian Mountains, Great Smoky Mountains National Park, Tennessee / North Carolina   LARRY ULRICH

“ Mountains are giant, restful, absorbent. You can heave your spirit into a mountain and the mountain will keep it, folded, and not throw it back as some creeks will. The creeks are the world with all its stimulus and beauty; I live there. But the mountains are home. ”

Annie Dillard,
Pilgrim at Tinker Creek

Pink azaleas and Linville Falls along the Blue Ridge Parkway, North Carolina   CARR CLIFTON

A boy and his bike and the stars and stripes in Atwood, Illinois   RICHARD HAMILTON SMITH

" *Summer is vacation time, sweet clover time, swing and see-saw time, watermelon time, swimming and picnic and camping and Fourth-of-July time . . . . It is fishing time, canoeing time, baseball time. It is, for millions of Americans, 'the good old summertime.'* "

Edwin Way Teale,
Journey into Summer

Girl Scouts united for fun in Richmond, Virginia   CATHERINE KARNOW

Silent humor at the Little Rock Zoo, Arkansas   MATT BRADLEY

Taking watermelons seriously in Tucson, Arizona
FRANK OBERLE / PHOTOGRAPHIC RESOURCES

Monmouth Plantation, built about 1818, in Natchez, Mississippi   MATT BRADLEY

Pink and white dogwood blossoms near Decatur, Alabama   ANNE HEIMANN

Sharing a summer secret—and giggles—in Baton Rouge, Louisiana CATHERINE KARNOW

Red fox pups sharing a moment near Roanoke, Virginia
STEPHEN J. KRASEMANN / DRK PHOTO

" *How the petals of a daisy all*
  gather to make one—
How the children of the
  summer join together to
  have fun. . . .
How they all belong together
Is how I'd like to be. *"*

Erika Laughlin, Grade 8,
Mandeville, Louisiana.
From "How They All Belong Together"
in the Young Writer's Contest.

A pastel day on the Jersey Shore, New Jersey   DAVID LORENZ WINSTON

Bucket brigade patrolling Bradenton Beach, Florida
PAUL E. CLARK/N. E. STOCK PHOTO

Exploring the shore of Chippewa Harbor on Lake Superior, Isle Royale National Park, Michigan   DANIEL J. COX

Putting for par by the Pacific, Molokai, Hawaii   ALLEN DEAN STEELE / STOCK SOUTH

National Volleyball Championships at Hermosa Beach, California   CATHERINE KARNOW

Lifting weights on Hermosa Beach, California   CATHERINE KARNOW

Tanning line at poolside, Honolulu, Hawaii   STEPHEN TRIMBLE

American freestyle, circa 1990s, Virginia Beach, Virginia   CATHERINE KARNOW

Cross-country skiers making tracks on fresh snow near Aspen, Colorado   ANNIE GRIFFITHS BELT

" *Winter has settled down over the Divide again; the season in which Nature recuperates, in which she sinks to sleep between the fruitfulness of autumn and the passion of spring.* "

Willa Cather,
O Pioneers!

Who needs hockey when you can have broomball?
Appleton, Wisconsin   RICHARD HAMILTON SMITH

Winter settling on the Continental Divide in the San Juan Mountains, Colorado   TOM TILL

Winter on Crater Lake, atop an ancient volcano, Crater Lake National Park, Oregon   GREG VAUGHN

White-tailed ptarmigan dressed for winter, Bob Marshall Wilderness, Montana   MICHAEL S. SAMPLE

Pure blue sky, pure white snow,
pure fun at Taos Ski Valley, New Mexico   KEN GALLARD

Multnomah Falls transformed into an icefall, Columbia River Gorge, Oregon   RUSSELL LAMB

Launching a flotilla of Halloween pumpkins in Marin County, California DAVID CAVAGNARO/DRK PHOTO

Autumn-colored dragonfly in North Carolina LARRY R. DITTO

Autumn at Glade Creek Grist Mill in Babcock State Park, Allegheny Mountains, West Virginia   LARRY ULRICH

False hellebore advancing spring at Upper Mosquito Lake in Sequoia National Park, California   CARR CLIFTON

Bald eagle soaring over the Chilkat Bald Eagle Refuge, Haines, Alaska   TOM MANGELSEN

> *It is the eagle active, soaring in a vast, windy sky on a day of brilliant sunshine, that becomes transcendently the symbol of all freedom . . . .*

Edwin Way Teale,
Wandering through Winter

Ending a day of fishing on Lake Minnewaska, Minnesota   GREG L. RYAN / SALLY A. BEYER

"We need the tonic of wildness.... At the same time that we are earnest to explore and learn all things, we require that all things be mysterious and unexplorable, that land and sea be infinitely wild, unsurveyed and unfathomed by us because unfathomable. We can never have enough of Nature."

Henry David Thoreau,
Walden

Sunset at Lake Durant, Adirondack Park and Preserve, New York CARR CLIFTON

Two generations fishing for cutthroat trout, Yellowstone National
Park, Montana / Wyoming / Idaho LINDA CAUBLE

Ruby-throated hummingbird, ruby-colored raspberry,
near Eagle River, Wisconsin
STEPHEN J. KRASEMANN / DRK PHOTO

"*A waterfall is like silver beads*
Tumbling off rocks, and if you
Watch long enough you will
wonder
Where it leads and what you'll
Find if you follow.

Its cool breeze is like a small
Hand brushing by your cheek.
You want it to come back and
Touch you again."

Kristina Beyer, Grade 6,
St. Paul, Minnesota.
From "Waterfall" in the
Young Writer's Contest.

White Oak Run cascading through White Oak Canyon, Shenandoah National Park, Virginia   WILLARD CLAY

Inspecting the Bay Bridge between San Francisco and Oakland, California   CURTIS MARTIN / PHOTOGRAPHIC RESOURCES

" ...the genius of the United States is not best or most in its executives or legislatures, nor in its ambassadors or authors or colleges or churches or parlors, nor even in its newspapers or inventors... but always most in the common people. "

Walt Whitman,
preface to Leaves of Grass

Grandpa's apprentice, Marin County, California   DAVID CAVAGNARO

Cheerful farmer near Poolesville, Maryland   CATHERINE KARNOW

Celebrating the fiftieth birthday of the Huntsville Museum of Art,
Huntsville, Alabama   ROB OUTLAW

Sharing a laugh in Highland County, Virginia CATHERINE KARNOW

Sculpting bronze art in Helena, Montana
GENE FISCHER

A living Statue of Liberty, New York City ANNIE GRIFFITHS BELT

Between fires in Livingston, Montana　AIUPPY PHOTOGRAPHS

Old Order Mennonite carriage, Caernarvon Township, Pennsylvania   ROBERT F. LEAHY

" *The United States is a country unique in the world because it was populated not merely by people who live in it by the accident of birth, but by those who willed to come here.* "

John Gunther,
Inside U.S.A.

A Cub Scout of America,
Los Angeles, California   CATHERINE KARNOW

Chinatown merchant, San Francisco, California
MARK & JENNIFER MILLER

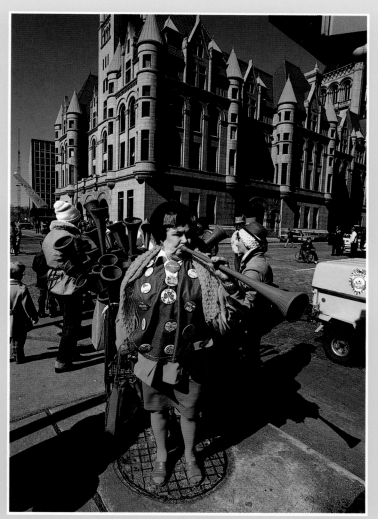

Tuning up for St. Patrick's Day Parade, St. Paul, Minnesota
ANNIE GRIFFITHS BELT

Between performances of the Ballet Folklorico,
Tucson, Arizona   MATT BRADLEY

Strumming in Central Park, New York City   CATHERINE KARNOW

Autumn sunset over the Grand Tetons and the Snake River, Grand Teton National Park, Wyoming   W. PERRY CONWAY

Bull moose, Yellowstone National Park,
Montana / Wyoming / Idaho   TOM MANGELSEN

Blue columbine, San Juan National
Forest, Colorado   LARRY ULRICH

*" Wilderness is the raw material out of which man has
hammered the artifact called civilization. "*

Aldo Leopold,
A Sand County Almanac

Roses flourishing at an abandoned homestead near Fort Bragg in northern California CARR CLIFTON

Six-foot-tall black dragon lilies and four-foot-tall admirer, Decorah, Iowa DAVID CAVAGNARO

" Every rose on the little tree
is making a different face at me.
Some look surprised when I go by;
others droop as if they were shy. . . .
Some have their heads thrown back to sing
and all the buds are listening.
I wonder if the gardener knows,
or if he calls each just a rose? "

Jamie Krause, Grade 8,
Cleveland, North Carolina.
From "The Little Rose Tree"
in the Young Writer's Contest.

Native bluebonnets and phlox near Gillett, Texas   WILLARD CLAY

The distinctive Big Sur coastline at Julia Pfeiffer Burns State Park, California   LARRY ULRICH

A mouth-watering lunch of plankton for a humpback whale off Portsmouth, New Hampshire   TED LEVIN

" *It tempted; it beckoned; it called to me,*
To that part of my soul I could not suppress.
It lodged deep within my heart, I confess,
The wildness, the glory, of the sea. "

Clarissa Martinez, Grade 8,
Bethesda, Maryland.
From ''The Sea'' in the
Young Writer's Contest.

Winter sun on El Capitan, a granite monolith above the Merced River in Yosemite National Park, California   JAMES RANDKLEV

The sun illuminates only the eye of the man, but shines into the eye and heart of the child. The lover of nature is he whose inward and outward senses are still truly adjusted to each other; who has retained the spirit of infancy even into the era of manhood.

Ralph Waldo Emerson,
Nature

Shining into the eye of an awestruck child in a grove of majestic redwoods, Yosemite National Park, California   TOM MYERS

Claret cup cactus blooming at Joshua Tree
National Monument, California   JEFF FOOTT

*"" For all the toll the desert takes
of a man it gives compensations, deep
breaths, deep sleep, and the communion
of the stars. ""*

Mary Austin,
The Land of Little Rain

Clearing after a rare winter snowstorm, Zion National Park, Utah   CHARLES GURCHE

The aptly named Maze area of Canyonlands National Park, Utah   BALLENGER / TULLEY

An oasis near the Grand Canyon—Havasu Falls on the Havasupai Indian Reservation, Arizona   LARRY ULRICH / DRK

Mountain lion, New Mexico   CHASE SWIFT

Herding longhorns at sunset in "cowboy country" near Fort Worth, Texas   BUDDY MAYS

There is an easy comfort given to believers of the Western dream, knowing that cowboys are, at this very moment, galloping around somewhere, roping sick stock, and sleeping out under the stars.

Kurt Markus,
Buckaroo

Taking a break from a wild-horse roundup near Shoshone, Idaho   DAVID STOECKLEIN

At the end of a dusty trail, near Oklahoma City, Oklahoma
RICHARD HAMILTON SMITH

Cowboy gear ready to go at the 63 Ranch,
Livingston, Montana   AIUPPY PHOTOGRAPHS

Bull rider's mental warm-up at the Intertribal Ceremonial Rodeo, Gallup, New Mexico   STEPHEN TRIMBLE

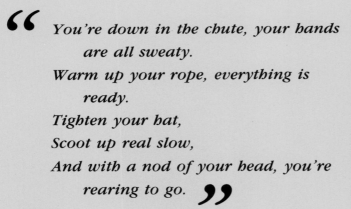

You're down in the chute, your hands
    are all sweaty.
Warm up your rope, everything is
    ready.
Tighten your hat,
Scoot up real slow,
And with a nod of your head, you're
    rearing to go.

Ryan Grandi, Grade 7,
Albuquerque, New Mexico.
From "Eight-Second Ride"
in the Young Writer's Contest.

Goat-tying at the College National Finals Rodeo,
Montana State University, Bozeman, Montana   WILLIAM R. SALLAZ

Rounding up horses near Tumalo, Oregon   LAURA HOUSE / VISIONS FROM NATURE

Waiting for the judges at the 4-H County Fair, Burley, Idaho   BOB FIRTH / FIRTH PHOTO BANK

Continuing a tradition at the Ala Moana Center in Honolulu, Hawaii   STEPHEN TRIMBLE

No alien land in all the world has any deep strong charm for me but that one, no other land could so longingly and so beseechingly haunt me, sleeping and waking, through half a lifetime, as that one has done. Other things leave me, but it abides; other things change, but it remains the same. For me its balmy airs are always blowing, its summer seas flashing in the sun; the pulsing of its surfbeat is in my ear . . . .

Mark Twain,
Mark Twain's Letters from Hawaii

Making new land, the Pu'u 'O'o rift eruption, Hawaii Volcanoes National Park, Kilauea, Hawaii   GREG VAUGHN

Diamond Head rising from the Pacific, Honolulu, Hawaii PETE SALOUTOS / PHOTOGRAPHIC RESOURCES

Racing the curl in Hawaii LARRY PIERCE / PHOTOGRAPHIC RESOURCES

Nanue Falls with flowering tulip trees and royal palms, Hamakua Coast, Hawaii   LARRY ULRICH / DRK PHOTO

Drilling for silver near Kellogg, Idaho   SCOTT SPIKER

" *A truly American sentiment recognizes the dignity of labor and the fact that honor lies in honest toil.* "

Grover Cleveland,
letter accepting nomination for the presidency,
August 18, 1884

Hay-bale brigade in southern Minnesota   ANNIE GRIFFITHS BELT

Where there's smoke there's a firefighter, St. Louis, Missouri   DOUG MINER / PHOTOGRAPHIC RESOURCES

Enjoying a patrol in San Francisco, California
GALEN ROWELL

Alfresco dining on the unfinished ninth floor,
Dallas, Texas   DOUG MILNER / DRK PHOTO

Talking over the day's work in the Red River Valley near Wahpeton, North Dakota   ANNIE GRIFFITHS BELT / DRK PHOTO

I am inclined to think that being a success is tied up very closely with being one's own kind of individual.

Eleanor Roosevelt,
You Learn by Living

Teamwork in Steamboat Springs, Colorado
FRANK OBERLE / PHOTOGRAPHIC RESOURCES

Fishing the Colorado River in the
Grand Canyon, Arizona   RON SANFORD

« America is rather like life.
You can usually find in it what
you look for . . . . It will probably
be interesting, and it is sure to be
large. »

E. M. Forster,
"The United States,"
in Two Cheers for Democracy

Evening light on the Grand Canyon from the South Rim, Grand Canyon National Park, Arizona   MARK MILLER

Too cool in front of the St. James Club on Sunset Boulevard, Los Angeles, California   CATHERINE KARNOW

Evening migration out of Los Angeles, California   PETE SALOUTOS / PHOTOGRAPHIC RESOURCES

Neon oasis in the desert, Las Vegas, Nevada   JOHN ELK III

Vietnamese family celebrating graduation at Tufts University, Medford, Massachusetts   FRANK SITEMAN / NE STOCK PHOTO

“ Education is our passport to the future, for tomorrow belongs to the people who prepare for it today. ”

Malcolm X,
Jet

Sharing the joys of reading, Los Angeles, California   CATHERINE KARNOW

A formula for the future, Edgewater High School in Orlando, Florida
BILL BACHMANN / NE STOCK PHOTO

Symbol of the last frontier, a grizzly bear patrolling the Alaskan tundra, Denali National Park   KIM HEACOX

" *We are a people born to the frontier. It has been a part of our thinking, waking, and sleeping since men first landed on this continent. The frontier is the line that separates the known from the unknown wherever it may be, and we have a driving need to see what lies beyond. It was this that brought people to America.* "

Louis L'Amour,
Frontier

Astronaut Bruce McCandless II enjoying the first untethered space walk, February 1984   COURTESY OF NASA

Washington Monument framed by cherry blossoms,
Washington, D.C.   SCOTT T. SMITH

The Capitol dome and streetlamp, Washington, D.C.
CATHERINE KARNOW

>   " *I believe that out of the whole body of our past, out of our differences, our quarrels, our many interests and directions, something has emerged that is itself unique in the world: America—complicated, paradoxical, bullheaded, shy, cruel, boisterous, unspeakably dear, and very beautiful.* "

John Steinbeck,
America and Americans

The U.S. Navy's Blue Angels in formation above the Patuxent River Naval Air Station, Maryland   THOMAS R. FLETCHER

Celebrating graduation at the U.S. Military Academy, West Point, New York   BILL FOLEY / STOCK SOUTH

The Lincoln Memorial, patrolled by a National Park Service ranger, Washington, D.C.   STEPHEN TRIMBLE / DRK PHOTO

Little Round Top, where Union forces turned back Confederates in the Battle of Gettysburg, Pennsylvania   SAM ABELL

Remembering the past in Tupelo, Mississippi   JACK OLSON

> *It is rather for us to be here dedicated to the great task remaining before us—that from these honored dead we take increased devotion to that cause for which they here gave the last full measure of devotion—that we here highly resolve that these dead shall not have died in vain—that this nation, under God, shall have a new birth of freedom—and that government of the people, by the people, for the people, shall not perish from the earth.*

Abraham Lincoln,
address at Gettysburg
November 19, 1863

The First Amendment at work in Washington, D.C.   DAVID LORENZ WINSTON

Congress shall make no law respecting an establishment of religion, or prohibiting the free exercise thereof; or abridging the freedom of speech, or of the press; or the right of the people peaceably to assemble, and to petition the Government for a redress of grievances.

First Amendment,
Constitution of the United States

Flag ceremony at Carswell Air Force Base, Fort Worth, Texas   DOUG MILNER / DRK PHOTO

Vietnam Veterans Memorial, Washington, D.C.   KIM HEACOX

" *The thing I like best about life today*
Is that I can say what I want to say.
Freedom is what I'm talking about.
I have freedom to yell and freedom to
    shout.
I have freedom of speech, I have
    freedom of choice.
I don't have to listen to a king raise his
    voice.
There's lots of freedom everywhere.
There's enough freedom for everyone to
    share. "

Justin Hatch, Grade 3,
Logandale, Nevada.
From "Life in America"
in the Young Writer's Contest.

Traditional boat building, San Juan Islands, Washington
FRANS LANTING / MINDEN PICTURES

Between the forge and the anvil near Fiddletown, California
TOM MYERS

" To the laborer in the sweat of his labor, the raw stuff on his anvil is an adversary to be conquered. . . . But to the laborer in repose, able for the moment to cast a philosophical eye on his world, that same raw stuff is something to be loved and cherished, because it gives definition and meaning to his life. "

Aldo Leopold,
A Sand County Almanac

Last nail of the day at the University of Idaho, Moscow, Idaho   SCOTT SPIKER

Weaving form and function in a Navajo rug, Santa Fe, New Mexico   STEPHEN TRIMBLE

Cheering the Georgia-Florida game at the Gator Bowl, Jacksonville, Florida   GORDON JOFFRION / STOCK SOUTH

" They say football is America's greatest game, but it's not. The greatest game in America is called opportunity. Football is merely a great expression of it. "

Joe Kapp,
quoted by James Lawton
in The All American War Game

Always looking for opportunities, Joe Montana of the
San Francisco 49ers   SCOTT CUNNINGHAM

Atlanta Braves' Oddibe McDowell beating the tag from Philadelphia's Ricky Jordan, Atlanta, Georgia   DAVID PERDEW / STOCK SOUTH

Learning baseball in L'Anse, Michigan   DON & PAT VALENTI / DRK PHOTO

> **" Whoever wants to know the heart and mind of America had better learn baseball. "**
>
> Jacques Barzun,
> God's Country and Mine

Breaking away at the Little 500 Bicycle Race, Indiana University, Bloomington, Indiana   DAVID PERDEW / STOCK SOUTH

Tennis ace Jennifer Capriati during the Federation Cup, Atlanta, Georgia
KEN HAWKINS / STOCK SOUTH

Start of the 140-mile Ironman Triathlon, Kailua-Kona, Hawaii   GREG VAUGHN

Floor routine at the 1989 Olympic Festival, Oklahoma City, Oklahoma   WILLIAM R. SALLAZ

Portrait of the Mother of Exiles   PETE SALOUTOS / PHOTOGRAPHIC RESOURCES

> *Here at our sea-washed, sunset gates shall stand*
> *A mighty woman with a torch, whose flame*
> *Is the imprisoned lightning, and her name*
> *Mother of exiles.*

Emma Lazarus,
The New Colossus

Celebrating the Fourth of July, 1986, after the restoration of the Statue of Liberty   BILL FOLEY / STOCK SOUTH

A blizzard of snow geese above the Delaware River estuary between Delaware and New Jersey   ROBERT PERRON

Surf fishing on Cape Cod, Massachusetts   ANNIE GRIFFITHS BELT / DRK PHOTO

Edge of the Atlantic at Lands End near Newport, Rhode Island   DAVID MUENCH

Collecting quahogs, the main ingredient for clam chowder,
on Nantucket Island, Massachusetts   CATHERINE KARNOW

Fertile contours of corn, oats, and alfalfa in southeast Minnesota   RICHARD HAMILTON SMITH

Man-sized soybeans, giant-sized corn near St. Charles, Missouri   FRANK OBERLE / PHOTOGRAPHIC RESOURCES

> " *The windy springs and the blazing summers, one after another, had enriched and mellowed that flat tableland; all the human effort that had gone into it was coming back in long, sweeping lines of fertility. The changes seemed beautiful and harmonious to me; it was like watching the growth . . . of a great idea.* "
>
> Willa Cather,
> My Antonia

Harvesting wheat on the rolling hills of the Palouse area in eastern Washington SCOTT SPIKER

Alternating rows of sunflowers and wheat in west-central North Dakota   ANNIE GRIFFITHS BELT

Pick of the pumpkins, Presque Isle, Maine   DOUGLAS MERRIAM

A meeting of minds in the South Dakota badlands
ANNIE GRIFFITHS BELT

133

Food for the body, feast for the eye, Decorah, Iowa
DAVID CAVAGNARO / DRK PHOTO

Floral farming: commercial tulip fields in Skagit County, Washington   CHARLES GURCHE

Gateway Arch and riverboats on the Mississippi River, St. Louis, Missouri   ANNIE GRIFFITHS BELT

❝ *The American, by nature, is optimistic. He is experimental, an inventor and a builder who builds best when called upon to build greatly.* **❞**

John F. Kennedy,
address in Washington, D.C.,
January 1, 1960

Looking for solutions in a San Francisco laboratory, California
TOM TRACY / PHOTOGRAPHIC RESOURCES

Industrial balancing act in Erlanger, Kentucky   JAMES R. FISHER / DRK PHOTO

A waterfall at Old Man's Cave State Park southeast of Columbus, Ohio   TOM TILL

Reflections in the Housatonic River near Cornwall Bridge, Connecticut   DAVID MUENCH

Trillium-lined trail in Selkirk Shores State Park north of Syracuse, New York   CARR CLIFTON

Nighttime light show—the aurora borealis—above a tent in the Alaska Range,
Alaska   SCOTT T. SMITH

" *The great grizzly bear*
Lifts his mighty head,
The white-tailed deer pricks his
Small ears to the sky
And knows that he is safe in
America. . . .
When the wild mustang of Wyoming
Whinnies into the darkness of the night,
That means I love America. "

Jedediah Brown, Grade 4,
Pinedale, Wyoming.
From ''Never Ending Sureness''
in the Young Writer's Contest.

Sunset in the Norse Peak Wilderness, Mount Baker-Snoqualmie National Forest, Washington   PAT O'HARA

Prairie vision, Badlands National Park, South Dakota   TOM BEAN / DRK PHOTO

> *The prairie sings to me in the forenoon and I know in the night I rest easy in the prairie arms, on the prairie heart.*
>
> **Carl Sandburg,**
> ''Prairie,'' in Complete Poems

Queen Anne's lace decorating the Oklahoma prairie
STEPHEN J. KRASEMANN / DRK PHOTO

Monument Rocks in eastern Kansas, landmark to wagon trains on the Butterfield Trail   DAVID MUENCH

Native grasslands of The Nature Conservancy's Flint Hills Preserve near Alma, Kansas   DAVID MUENCH

Whitetail fawn and coneflowers at The Nature Conservancy's Tallgrass Prairie Preserve, Oklahoma   HARVEY PAYNE

" *As I walked along the ridge I looked out across the plains, the hills barely rippling in the sun, each hill so small in the distance. I began to feel a beat, a rhythm, like the beat of my heart but much, much bigger.... It was the beat of the plains, the hills and the draws and the flats, and yesterday and today and tomorrow....* "

Hal Borland,
High, Wide and Lonesome

Scotts Bluff, landmark for emigrants along the Oregon Trail, Nebraska   WILLARD CLAY

Living symbol of the plains, bison and calf at the Wichita Mountains National Wildlife Refuge, Oklahoma   MICHAEL S. SAMPLE

Roseate spoonbills in breeding plumage, Everglades National Park, Florida   LARRY LIPSKY

" *Lying in comfort by the sea, you receive gratefully the gift of the sun, the gift of the South. This is true seduction.* **"**

E. B. White,
The Points of My Compass

A patch of cabbage palms at dawn, Big Cypress National Preserve, Florida   CARR CLIFTON

Natural neon in a big empty, the Maze district of Canyonlands National Park, Utah   GARY LADD

" I prefer the absences and the big empties, where the wind ricochets from sand grain to mountain. I prefer the crystalline dryness and an unadulterated sky strewn from horizon to horizon with stars. I prefer the raw edges and the unfinished hems of the desert landscape. "

Ann Zwinger,
The Mysterious Lands

Evening light on the gypsum dunes of White Sands National Monument, New Mexico   DENNIS & MARIA HENRY

Aspen forest accented by blue columbines, Gunnison National Forest, Colorado   WILLARD CLAY

❝ *The forests of America, however slighted by man, must have been a great delight to God, because they were the best He ever planted.* ❞

John Muir,
quoted by John Gunther in Inside U.S.A.

Emerald expanse of conifer trees in Bighorn National Forest, Wyoming   TOM BEAN

Appalachian Mountains from Cumberland Gap National Historic Park, Kentucky / Tennessee / Virginia   TOM TILL

Whitetail buck near San Antonio, Texas
CLAUDE STEELMAN / TOM STACK & ASSOCIATES

Bald cypress knee-deep in Trussum Pond State Preserve, Delaware   DAVID MUENCH

Turret Arch from the South Window, Arches National Park, Utah   LARRY ULRICH

Oak Creek and Cathedral Rock, Coconino National Forest, Arizona   LARRY ULRICH

Morning light on the Chisos Mountains and Rio Grande in Big Bend National Park, Texas   WILLARD CLAY

" It is good to realize that, if love and peace can prevail on earth, and if we can teach our children to honor nature's gifts, the joys and beauties of the outdoors will be here forever. "

Jimmy Carter,
An Outdoor Journal

Viewing 14,410-foot Mount Rainier from Tolmie Peak in
Mount Rainier National Park, Washington   PAT O'HARA

The edge of day on 11,012-foot Gallatin Peak, Gallatin National Forest, Montana   MICHAEL S. SAMPLE

Sunset at Crescent Beach, Ecola State Park, Oregon   WILLARD CLAY

Ronald McDonald Children's Charities®

Helping children in all neighborhoods around the globe achieve healthier, happier, and more productive lives is the fundamental goal of Ronald McDonald Children's Charities.

A not-for-profit organization, Ronald McDonald Children's Charities supports other not-for-profit groups whose programs directly benefit children. Social awareness programs that teach children what it's like to have a disability. Educational activities that encourage youngsters to read, write, and be creative. Health care programs that improve the quality of life for children. Even fulfilling a simple request to provide transportation for an organization so that youngsters can get to the doctor, attend a counseling session, or participate in a recreation hour. As the grassroots children's charity, Ronald McDonald Children's Charities' goal is to fund and support efforts that will lift kids to a better tomorrow.

Ronald McDonald Children's Charities was created in 1984 in memory of McDonald's Corporation founder Ray A. Kroc, who held a long-time belief of "giving back" to the communities in which we live.

That philosophy covers a lot of territory for Ronald McDonald Children's Charities. Since its inception, the charity has contributed more than $34 million to more than 900 organizations whose programs specialize in health care and medical research, including Ronald McDonald House; education and the arts; and civic and social service activities. Grants are approved by the Board of Trustees, comprised of health professionals; business and civic leaders; and officers, directors, and licensees of McDonald's Corporation.

Recipients of Ronald McDonald Children's Charities grants are as diverse as education for latch-key children, direct services for the families and children of military personnel affected by a crisis overseas, an arts program for handicapped school-aged children, child abuse prevention, substance abuse prevention, and a cultural and educational outreach program for elementary school children.

For five consecutive years, Ronald McDonald Children's Charities has given substantial grants to the Young Writer's Contest Foundation, whose goal is to encourage children to read and write. Currently, Young Writer's is the only nationwide writing contest for first through eighth graders. The winning entries are printed in the *Rainbow Collection: Stories and Poetry by Young People* and distributed nationally.

This year, however, the Young Writer's Contest has been expanded and enhanced. Students were asked to write on the subject of America, and their winning entries, including the Grand Prize entry, are featured in this unique book.

In observance of International Literacy Year and to show our commitment to the campaign against illiteracy, Ronald McDonald Children's Charities and Falcon Press have awarded $30,000 in contributions to schools for the purchase of reading materials.

Ronald McDonald Children's Charities is proud to support this effort, knowing that our partnership with the Young Writer's Contest Foundation and Falcon Press will make inroads in the campaign against illiteracy.

young writer's contest foundation

The Young Writer's Contest Foundation is a nonprofit, tax-exempt organization dedicated to encouraging and highlighting the importance of language-arts skills. To achieve this goal, we sponsor an annual writing contest for first through eighth graders throughout the nation. This year, we received about 18,000 entries. The following 100 winners were selected based on the content, grammar, creativity, originality, and literary merit of their work.

The poems, stories, and essays that we've received during the seven-year life of the contest have allowed us to glimpse into the classrooms, homes, and communities of thousands of young people. It has been a treasured experience, and we salute the educators and families who have so obviously provided the patient guidance and the nurturing environment that motivate youngsters to write.

Writing is communication that endures. We may not always enjoy the process of writing—or the discipline it requires—but we do love having written. We preserve writing in scrapbooks, frame it under glass, tie it up with ribbon, and stash it in safe places. We protect writing; we want the thoughts behind the writing to live on—whether the work is our own or someone else's.

This special section of *America on My Mind* is full of precious words that record forever some of the events, feelings, and dreams of the six- to thirteen-year-olds who wrote them. Because they are written, they will endure. The Young Writer's Contest is deeply grateful to Ronald McDonald Children's Charities and Falcon Press Publishing Co. for joining us in our efforts to recognize and encourage America's young writers.

Kathie Janger
Executive Director
Young Writer's Contest Foundation

(Contest winners arranged in alphabetical order by state.)

Granddaddy

Every time I walked into the house, Granddaddy was sitting in his chair reading the newspaper. I would always go over and hug him because he liked to be hugged. He was fun to be around and had nice compliments for me. In fact, he never said anything bad about anyone. Granddaddy was a quiet, good-natured man and enjoyed having friends and family around him.

When I think about Granddaddy, I remember all the things he liked to do. Every day he went out and put food in all his birdfeeders, and then watched the birds come and eat it. He would tell me what kinds of birds were perched on the feeders. Granddaddy read a lot and worked all the crossword puzzles in the newspapers. He also liked to watch ballgames on television and kept up with his favorite teams. Daddy would always talk with him about sports. One of the neatest things about Granddaddy was how he peeled an apple. He would begin at the top, cutting just the peeling around the apple until nothing was left but the perfectly peeled apple and one long spiral peeling. He would be so proud that he had not wasted any of the apple.

One of my favorite things is to hear stories about Granddaddy. When he was young he had a dairy farm, and he would go there every day and count his cows. Can you believe he named every one of his cows? My mother can remember going to his farm to play and watch the cows being milked when she was about my age. Granddaddy also sold eggs he had gathered at his house. A lot of his friends would come to buy them. That must have been a lot of eggs to keep up with!

Granddaddy died this summer. He had lived a long, wonderful life. I was sad he was gone and knew that I would miss him, but there is one thing I will never forget about him. When I saw him in the hospital the day he died, he hugged me and wouldn't let me go for a long time. That made me feel very special to him and happy. He must have loved me very much.

Allison Ivey, Grade 4
Teacher: Sheryll S. Wolfe
Academy of Science & Foreign Language
Huntsville, Alabama

Untitled

Tenseness,
Silence,
Waiting,
He looks behind him,
All clear.
His hand is sweating inside his glove.
He positions his fingers.
Carefully he measures the distance
Between him
And his goal.
Then he pitches a fast accurate throw
And hears the umpire call,
"Strike!"
He readies himself for the next pitch,
And throws.
Crack!
The shortstop hears the
Sound
Of the bat.
The ball is coming toward him.
He extends himself upward,
Stretching,
Reaching,
One more inch,
He feels the ball fall solidly
Into his mitt.
The shortstop
Flips
The ball to the second
Baseman.
He steps on the bag.
Quickly and deliberately,
He whips the ball out,
And pelts it down
To the waiting catcher
At home plate.
The runner is nearly there.
He starts to slide,
Stretching,
Reaching,
One more inch.
He gropes for the base.
His fingers meet the ball,
Firmly locked
Within the catcher's grasp.
Triple play.
The game
Is over.

Gail Burger, Grade 6
Teacher: Jan Flanders
Rogers Park Elementary School
Anchorage, Alaska

The Hill

The rolling golden-brown carpet reflects the light
Of the disappearing sun just minutes before night.

Twisting branches cast a deep lonely shadow
Against giant guardians of the lake by the meadow.

A determined breeze reaches down with its icy
    breath
And whispers to crisp, clinging leaves of their
    approaching death.

Melanie Kuntz, Grade 7
Teacher: Margaret O'Bert
Barcelona Elementary School
Glendale, Arizona

The Little Princess

Once upon a time there was a Little Princess who had lots of friends. She liked playing with her father the king and doing stuff around the castle.

One day they heard about a great dragon that came to one of the villages of the kingdom, eating all the people. The king sent his men out to fight the dragon, but every time they went out, some never came back.

One day the Little Princess and the children who were her friends decided they would go out and fight the dragon. That night, when everyone was asleep, the children went out of the castle. They walked along the bank of a nearby creek until they saw the dragon. The dragon was up in the sky flying and didn't see them.

The children decided they would get a long rope and tie it to a humongous stone the size of a large room. They fixed the rope through a tall tree and pulled the stone up into the top of the tree. When the dragon came to get them, they could unhook the rope and drop the stone on him.

The children were about to fall asleep when they heard the dragon coming. They waited until it was under the rock. They pulled the rope and the humongous stone fell on the dragon and crushed him.

The children went back to the castle where their moms and dads were and brought them to see the dragon. The king and his men made sure the dragon was dead. They decided to eat the dragon for their supper.

The Little Princess was a heroine throughout the kingdom for leading the children against the dragon.

Tory Beth Hodges, Grade 1
Teacher: John Hodges
Alpena Public School
Alpena, Arkansas

Understanding

Knowledge is a mighty thing
To have in the hand,
But I would trade it all
If I could only understand.

Karen Paik, Grade 8
Teacher: Lida Lim
Burlingame Intermediate School
Burlingame, California

Spiked Swords of Snow

The mountains pierce the sky with spiked swords of
    snow.
The sun sparkles through them with a ruby-colored
    shimmer.
Eagles glide through the glen below,
While birds chirp their enlightening tune.

Hikers are whistling while they wisk up the steep
    mountainside,
And chipmunks dash off with the first sound of
    movement.
The trees stare down upon the earth with a wilted
    feeling of worthlessness,
But as soon as a bird comes flying in to feed its
    chicks,
The trees smile and seem to skip as they sway in the
    breeze.

Boulders squat and watch over the tiny insects that
    build a home below them.
A waterfall watches from behind the trees
And then spots a starer and disappears.
The hikers have reached the top
Of the mountain that pierces the sky with spiked
    swords of snow.

John Niekrasz, Grade 8
Teacher: Jerelyn Johnson
Bonita Vista Junior High School
Chula Vista, California

A Poem for Two About the Night

Stars   Solar Powered Vehicle

We are drops of paint.
The night is our canvas.

        The sun promotes darkness.
        Sunset stops my swift stir.

The eve offers darkness.
We can shine
As a sun before dawn.

        I can enact my evening
            motto:
        ''Freeze''

The eve offers freedom
to dart through the
    sparkling skies.

        The night ends my
            freedom.
        Stillness is an unruffled
            gesture.

When night ends its
    reign,
Frequently we fade,
Like falling fortune.

        When night ends its reign,
        My thrust advances.
        I begin to agitate.

Faded.

        Zoom.

We are dewdrops,
The night is our lawn.

        The night is a witch.
        I dwell in her overnight
            cemetery.

Sparkle, dazzle.

        Isolation

Night is an open door.

        Night is a closed door.

Every

        Evening

No matter

        Our opinion

We return to nocturne.

        We return to nocturne.

David Susman, Grade 5
Teacher: Carla Newton
Nueva School
Hillsborough, California

All I See Is a Clock

I've got a report (it's due tomorrow),
But instead I sit in sorrow,
And all I see is a clock,
Tick Tock,
It's four o'clock!

It must be written on some story,
But instead I sit without glory,
All I see is a clock,
Tick Tock,
It's six o'clock!

Oh, great! Now it's dark,
And still my pencil's made no mark,
All I see is a clock,
Tick Tock,
It's eight o'clock!

Now I'm really starting to fear,
For my bedtime is very near,
All I see is a clock,
Tick Tock,
It's ten o'clock!

Now my parents are full of steam,
But literally that's not what I mean,
All I see is a clock,
Tick Tock,
It's twelve o'clock!

Now it's early in the morning,
Still my story has no starting,
All I see is a clock,
Tick Tock,
It's two o'clock!

So here I sit broken-hearted,
Tried to write but barely started,
All I see is a clock,
Tick Tock,
It's four o'clock!

What is this? My mind is clear!
No more tick tocks in my ear!
I won't fret,
I won't fear,
My report is done; it's right here!

Devon Nunes, Grade 6
Teacher: Tom Alessi
Meadow Park School
Irvine, California

Orphan Wolf

The blazing sun streaked across the morning sky, its shimmering rays piercing through a narrow passage of the dark cave where a mother wolf lay with her newborn pup. A curious mouse scampered across the floor, holding the she-wolf's attention. Light gray and brown downy fur protruded from the pup's skin, forming a densely matted covering. Outside, the dew glistened lightly on the scattered mounds of greenery. A blue jay shrieked loudly as the mother wolf forced her baby to his feet. His flimsy legs wobbled and swayed as he inched forward. Even though he trembled and quaked, anyone could see that he would grow to be a strong runner. Sharp ivory teeth and fangs lined the outside of the baby wolf's jaws, giving him a cute yet fierce appearance.

Suddenly an alarming scent drifted into the pup's wet nostrils. A gruesome figure could be seen approaching through the trees. The pup could see his mother's lips curled back in a dangerous snarl as he fled to shelter in the nearby cave. The figure lifted something long, and with a reverberating blast, the mother wolf collapsed into a silent, motionless heap. As he stood whimpering with his tail hanging limply behind him, the pup sensed that his mother would no longer be there to guide and protect him. With a heavy heart he fell into a troubled sleep.

The next morning the baby wolf was startled out of a deep sleep. He awoke to see a man glancing back and forth, first at him then at his lifeless mother. After being coaxed out of the cave with a tempting piece of meat, the hungry pup slowly followed the man into a small clearing in the woods.

The sun was high in the sky when the two companions reached the man's cabin. The nervous pup hesitated at the entrance but was lured inside by another piece of tender meat. Once inside, the wolf was made comfortable in a softly cushioned basket. He cautiously gazed around the strange room, wondering what would happen next.

The man and pup lived happily together in the isolated cabin for several months. Day after day they walked, played, slept, and ate together, and a very deep bond of friendship developed between them. The man knew that the wolf should not be held captive and protected much longer and had to be set free. He feared that the baby wolf would soon lose his natural instincts for survival in the wild.

Tears welled up in the man's eyes as he mournfully opened the door to let the wolf out. The pup hesitantly emerged from the cabin, and after one last parting glance, he bounded off to seek food and shelter in the vast and lonely wilderness.

Even as time passes, both man and wolf think fondly of their brief time together and remember the strong kinship that developed between man and animal.

Rachel Lev, Grade 5
Teacher: Cynthia Phelps / Stacy Rolfe
Santiago Hills Elementary School
Irvine, California

Memories

Memories
Like silent birds
Flying above the seas
Of my mind,
Appearing, and then
Vanishing into clouds of thought.
They fly
Over the dark plains of the future,
Or glide gracefully
On sweet wings
To return to their distant homes
Of the past.

Carie Yonekawa, Grade 8
Teacher: Deeni Schoenfeld
Dorris-Eaton School
Walnut Creek, California

The Secret

Woven into words of whisper
        Sailing off a silent tongue,
A secret told in the ear of wisdom
        Memories made to someone young.

Note the detail of this magic
        Silken dreams yet to come,
Not just talking, mumbling nonsense
        Special detail, beautifully sung.

Listen carefully to this secret
        If you want to know its meaning,
All that's needed is a wish
        Of loving, needing, dreaming. . . .

Sarah Joseph, Grade 5
Teacher: Charles R. Clark
Westlake Hills Elementary School
Westlake Village, California

Flowers from a Poet

I am a poet of flowers.
Even my name is a flower.

In the spring I bloom
And my words are iris
Of a royal sparkling blue.

My lavender violets are sounds
Like a harp in spring
Playing songs that dance for you.

The winds blow pansies about
And I sway in the breeze
Moving gently fro and to.

Sometimes my daisy petals fall
To the soft spring ground
And my colors flow anew.

As an evening primrose
My thoughts are of longing
But my sharp thorns are few.

I am writing this poem
On my wet new leaves
My ink is morning dew.

I am a poet of flowers.
Even my name is a flower: Lily.

Lily Adam, Grade 3
Teacher: Andrea Watson
The Forest Lyceum
Denver, Colorado

Wind

I can hear the wind.

Listen to it clanging, banging,
Rattling at the window demanding
To be let in.

I can hear the wind.

One tree's branch is shaking, breaking,
And then falling
Onto the soft earth.

I can hear the wind.

The wind is rolling, strolling,
And then gently blowing
Away.

Now
I can't hear the wind.

Now
The wind is
Gone.

Margot Simpson, Grade 4
Teacher: Susan Kasper
Wolcott Elementary School
West Hartford, Connecticut

Fog

Fog wraps a lady's face in a damp gray veil,
Confusing her as to which way to go.
Suddenly she is shut in a dank, dark prison cell.
Then the gentle sun lifts the misty mesh
And twinkles at the relieved woman,
Who now saunters on her way.

Erica Sweet, Grade 5
Teacher: Andrea Cunningham-Pahl
Pomfret Community School
Pomfret Center, Connecticut

Over the Rainbow

Everyone loves rainbows. They are cheerful and colorful—but I found a rainbow that is all white. It's my Dorset ewe lamb, Rainbow.

Last year, after raising my 4-H market lamb, I couldn't wait to get a ewe lamb I could keep! I picked her out when she was three weeks old. She was so cute and so white. I counted the days till she could leave her mother.

Finally, I got to bring Rainbow home! She was still so cute, so white, but SO stubborn. Every time I would get Rainbow's halter and walk up to her very slowly, talking sweetly, she would drop to the ground. She would lie down flat, and I would have to pull, push, beg, and finally get my dad to get her out of the pen.

The Delaware State Fair came fast. Remember Dorothy singing, "Somewhere over the rainbow, bluebirds fly...?" Well, over my Rainbow were the eyes of the Sheep Judge. It was the Junior Showmanship class. For those of you who are "non-sheep show-ers," the rules sound fairly simple. Keep your sheep's feet and legs square under your sheep, keep your eye on the judge, and follow directions.

Rainbow didn't like the rules; she thought this was boring. She wanted action. One minute we were standing in line, and the next thing I knew she was running with me into the center of the ring. Then she stopped so fast I went flying over the Rainbow and into the sawdust. This was not Kansas! Well, I had to get back up still holding Rainbow's head and neck—and my tears—and get back in line. It helped some when the judge said I didn't lose my cool.

At the Queen Anne County Fair, in the Dorset ewe lamb class, Rainbow was great and took first place. This meant she could go into the Dorset Champion Ewe class. I could only get all of Rainbow's four feet under her two times the whole class. I was so mad!

At the Maryland State Fair, Rainbow was great for me, but she flipped my mom and gave her a bloody knee.

I believe I started this story with "I couldn't wait to get my own ewe lamb...." Well, she wasn't always sunshine, and we had a little rain, but that is what it takes for a rainbow, and I love her anyway!

Sarah Passwaters, Grade 5
Teacher: Joanne Jones
Woodbridge Elementary School
Greenwood, Delaware

Message

I saw the night, her tall figure gliding silently, letting loose her silky black hair as a curtain of darkness over her world. Her luminous gray eyes grow sad as she sees the clouds of smog choking the delicate light of the stars. She sighs as she dips a long finger into the icy water, only to find it covered with puddles of thick black oil. I feel her breath on my face, her voice pleading urgently, "Please, do something."

As the dawn peers cautiously over the hilltops, night hurries away, gathering up her velvety hair as a single teardrop falls from her eye. Not many nights left, she thinks. Not enough time before the smog suffocates the music of the stars or drowns out the clean pure beams of the tiny pinpricks of light. Not enough time before oil chokes the smooth water in its ugliness. The minutes sift through our fingers like sand, and there is not enough time before the world is engulfed with blackness.

But wait, a single star cuts through the inky sky, a point of joy guiding hope. Dreams, love, and faith, like a path through a thorny, winding forest, are the only guides through these perilous times. A rainbow nearly blinds with its splendor, and the whisper of God echoes in our ears. His breath cools us from the furnace of our fears, and the Earth cradles us like a pillow, comforting us and wiping away our tears. Slowly, we curl up and wait for a peaceful sleep to descend and clear our minds of life's problems. Wearily, we lie amidst a dream.

Night smiles, knowing she has shown us the beauty of our country, our world. It is a beauty we must strive to restore and retain.

Erin Butler, Grade 8
Teacher: Joyce Walker
Rock Lake Middle School
Longwood, Florida

Never to Forget

I sit here today and write this essay not for me, but for others, so I and everyone else will never forget. Now, you shall ask me what, what should we never forget? And I will say, "Today."

Today was the dedication of the statue and the Holocaust Memorial. Elie Weisel spoke in honor of the six million Jews who died. My mother took me, and as my mother was walking with me she saw a man carrying a sign that said that he was left on the doorstep of a house (during the Holocaust) by his parents to save his life. The sign said that he was still looking for his parents. My mother told me what she had seen. Then she leaned her head on my shoulder and cried. I knew that going on the March of the Living two years ago had made a deep impression in her heart, so I just let her cry as much as she wanted to.

Later on, while we were listening to all the speakers, my mother noticed a number tattooed on an old lady's arm, and my mother nudged me. After that, wherever I looked I saw those blue numbers and each one I saw, I thought of the other thousands that also had once had those horrible numbers engraved in their arms. As Elie Weisel said, slowly, first a family, then a town, then a city, then a country, slowly they turned from names to numbers and then slowly, slowly, to nothingness.

It was hot at the Memorial. All the old people, men and women, were fainting from dehydration and sorrow, dropping off one by one like flies, just as it must have happened during the Holocaust. But they were here to remember. They didn't care about anything else. Girls and boys from the Hebrew Academy, my school, went around with ice and water, giving it out to the old people. Most of us stayed there not for our sake, but for the sake of the six million.

As we left I thought very hard about all I had seen. Now we were on our way to "Shalom 90," an Israeli dance group. I thought to myself that this isn't for my sake, it's so that I and all the other B'nai Israel should make up for all that the six million missed. The twelve- and thirteen-year-olds who never went on a date, the fifteen- and sixteen-year-olds who would never grow up to get married, the six- and seven-year-olds who never learned how to read and write and study Torah.

Take advantage of your life and enjoy it. This generation, this B'nai Israel, is free and alive, as they say: Am Yisrael Chai.

Rena Bunder, Grade 6
Teacher: Arlene Fishbein
Rabbi A. S. Gross Hebrew Academy
Miami Beach, Florida

Requiem

Its marvelously speckled coat
And big, gleaming eyes—
A sign of blissful
Immaturity,
It leaps through the dense woods,
Graceful and limber—
A skater dancing on
Cool ice.
Its nose quivers—
The smell of flowers
Too fragrant and aromatic.
Its ears perk up—
The song of a cheerful lark
Comforting and peaceful.
A good creature who knows no
Worry,
A special creature—
A creature whose brilliant beauty
Reflects the true serenity and inner peace
Of his soul.
Destined to live
Forever,
But destined
To die.
A figurehead in a cheap pub,
A tawny coat pinned up on a mahogany wall,
An expensive jacket in Macy's,
His innocence and youthfulness—
A crumpled mass of fur beneath a pile of
Dried leaves.
Yet,
He will never know.
Gayly, he bounds through a meadow
Plucking at
Emerald grass,
Lost in a world of purity,
A world of goodness,
A world of hope.

Sonesh Chainani, Grade 8
Teacher: Richard Peccie
Ransom-Everglades Middle School
Miami, Florida

Sometimes

I'm blind, but I don't always mind.
I have a dog to lead me around, to new places that
have
Lots of scents and sounds,
Some new, some familiar.

For blindness, there is no cure.
But I don't always mind.
Although sometimes, sometimes,
I long to see the new movie that people rave about
Instead of just hearing it.
Sometimes, I want to see the soft flowers,
Instead of just smelling them.

But most of all, I sometimes just want to see!
To some people, seeing is just a normal thing that
is taken
For granted,
But to people like me, those who can see have a
special
Ability.
People are scared of me, they act strange around
me just
Because I'm different in one way.

I'm different because I'm blind, but I don't always
mind,
Except sometimes.
Sometimes I dream that I can see, but then I come
back to
Reality, the dark, unseeing reality.
I'm blind, but I don't always mind.
Except sometimes.

Sara Henderson, Grade 6
Teacher: Donna Day
Venice Area Middle School
Venice, Florida

A Different World

The sun rose just above the horizon. I sat there looking at the last Wisconsin sunrise I would ever see. There isn't anything more beautiful than a Wisconsin sunrise, I thought as the tears rolled down my face.

"Tiffany, hurry up and get dressed. The movers will be here in ten minutes," my mother yelled. I'm sick of being rushed, I thought. Besides, I don't care if the movers come. The sooner they get here, the sooner we have to leave.

I had just finished getting dressed when the doorbell rang. Oh, no, the movers are here. It's really happening. Go away, movers, go away, I screamed in my mind. At the door I found my best friend, Page, not the movers after all.

"I came over to give this to you and to say goodbye," Page said. She handed me a small white box. Inside were a pair of small, heart-shaped crystal earrings. That was enough to start the tears again. We talked for awhile, but there really wasn't much left to say. I couldn't believe that I would never see her again. She told me that she would come to Georgia to visit me, but deep in my heart I knew that this would be the last time I ever saw Page. I watched her walk down my driveway, feeling like it was the end of the world. I would never have a friend like Page again.

Suddenly I saw the moving van coming up the drive. It seemed so big, like a monster coming to take my belongings. I hoped it would take them a long time, but in a short while the house was bare. I went to my room one last time. Even though it was empty, it was still my room. It always would be, because it was filled with my memories.

"Come on, everybody. Get in the car. We're off!" my dad yelled. Reluctantly, I got into the car. How could he be so excited? I wondered. As we backed down the driveway, everyone was silent. I watched our house as it faded into the distance. There goes my whole life, I thought.

As we headed south out of Wisconsin, I started to panic. What if no one likes me at the new school? What if I never have a friend again? What if I never see snow again? I was driving myself crazy, but I couldn't stop. I knew my problems were just beginning.

Hours later we drove across the border into Georgia. The sun was just rising over the mountains. It was pretty—almost as beautiful as a Wisconsin sunrise. Maybe it wouldn't be too bad here, I thought. Maybe it's not the end of the world, just a different world.

Tiffany Engel, Grade 5
Teacher: Ellen Miller
Belwood School
Calhoun, Georgia

Patriotism

Patriotism—love for our country and an unending
        devotion to it—is the good and right thing
        that binds America together.
Images of patriotism flash before our eyes like
        lightning daily.

The sun gleaming through majestic American flags as
        they gallantly snap and sway over green
        grass and gray tombstones in a national
        cemetery on Veteran's Day.
People hanging over highway overpasses yelling and
        whooping words of encouragement to
        young soldiers on their way to a world a
        million miles away.
American Olympic gold medal winners' voices
        breaking and eyes glistening as they hail
        their flag and sing their national anthem in
        front of the world.
The soldiers at Iwo Jima, though exhausted, raising
        their flag as artillery rings in their ears,
        smoke stings their nostrils, and blasts of
        fire fill the air.
Veterans, some upright, some handicapped, some
        slumped in wheelchairs, saluting the strains
        of "The Star Spangled Banner" as they
        float through the still air.
Baseball players, dressed in their unsoiled whites,
        their cleats resting on the vivid green
        grass, removing their caps and placing
        them over their hearts as the singer and
        the organist key up to salute their country.
The stark blackness of the Vietnam Veterans
        Memorial matching the mournful
        countenance of the respectful people who
        file past the infinite sandblasted names.
Flags plastered on rustic country mailboxes and red,
        white, and blue streamers fluttering like
        doves on car radio antennas in honor of
        the U.S. servicemen in the Middle East.

P
  a
    r
      i
        o
          t
            i
              s
                m

is America at its best.
May it always remain that way.

Jeffrey C. Fallis, Grade 8
Teacher: Margaret Wingate
Pine Mountain Middle School
Kennesaw, Georgia

Why?

Roses are so beautiful.
Why do they have to die?
I know it seems silly,
But I'm still wondering why.

They start their lives as buds
So elegant and fair,
Then burst into bloom with a scent so fragrant
I could float in the air.

Several flowers to a bush
Like stars in a peaceful sky,
So vivid and colorful,
They dazzle my eyes.

So perfect and dainty
Now I think I know—
A rose must leave us to make room
For another to grow.

Julie Snow, Grade 6
Teacher: Margaret Jambor
Hawaii Prep Academy
Kamuela, Hawaii

The Wolf

Silently as a feather falls to the earth,
It runs through the woods
With the speed of the wind
And the beauty of the dawn.

By day it sleeps peacefully,
By night it hunts for food
With the gracefulness of a dancer,
But with the strength of a bear.

In the forest or in the Arctic,
It struggles to survive
With the cunningness of a fox
And the playfulness of a squirrel.

It is a living legend,
The wolf.

Julia Price, Grade 6
Teacher: Paula Hochstetler
Washington School
Rexburg, Idaho

Small Towns

I was born in and live in a small town. I live in the country outside of Grangeville, Idaho. There are only 3,000 people in Grangeville. We live 200 miles from the nearest big city. I have visited some big cities and have read about them. Also, my father has told me about big cities. He was raised in New York and Los Angeles. I would rather live in a small town than a big city.

People care about each other in small towns. My mom tells me that when my twin sister and I were born, it was announced on the radio and many people came to see us. The neighbors put pink flags out on our lawn to welcome us home. Small towns are safe places to grow up in. We don't have much crime so you don't have to be afraid. Every person in this town knows each other. The bad part is if you don't behave, your parents will find out. My dad says he has a hundred spies.

I go to a small school called Grangeville Elementary. In our school I get a good education because I have a teacher who cares about me. We don't have fancy places to eat, shopping malls, or escalators. But we do have a prairie filled with farms and a beautiful forest with elk and deer.

I know there are lots of fun things to do in a big city, but there are still fun things to do in a small town. In the summer, I go camping and fishing. In the fall, I help my dad's friend, Pat Long, harvest wheat. I ride in the combine, but the best part is jumping in the back of the truck and eating the raw wheat. In the winter, I go skiing and sledding.

The worst part of living in a small town is leaving it when you grow up.

Maureen FitzMaurice, Grade 2
Teacher: Judy Wayenberg
Grangeville Elementary School
Grangeville, Idaho

The Blankness of Mind

Like a recently washed chalkboard,
Like a new sketch pad before the images of the artist
     bring it to life,
There are times when my mind is a total blank.
No daydreams intrude it,
No thoughts of yesteryear clutter it,
No attacks from the present penetrate it.
For a few moments my mind rests in its hammock of
     blankness.
It is not a frightening or lonely time.
Nevertheless, there is some sort of comfort to it.
The kind of comfort young children have when they
     think
That they are protected from everything.
A blank mind is no reason for teachers to scream....
Young adults need the moment to restore and revive
Themselves from the crush of thought.

Ian Arsenault, Grade 8
Teacher: Stephen Littell
Washburne School
Winnetka, Illinois

The Cave

I am a cave.
My eyes are boulders.
My nose is a dent.
My teeth are stalactites.
The river is my tongue.
A diamond is my brain.
I am warning you, I am crabby
And if you come in
I will swallow you.

Derrick F. Crooks, Grade 5
Teacher: Rohn Peterson
Gurnee Grade School
Gurnee, Illinois

Way Out West

Tall prairie grasses
Hypnotize cowboys on long journeys.
Distant mountains
Reach to touch puffy white pillows.

The setting sun draws swirls
Like crayons in the sky.
Prickly green monstrous hands appear
After dusty days.

Hardy rugged cowboys stand 'round the crackling
    campfire.
Grim tales are shared as
They eat their feast.
Sly coyotes creep about beyond the covered wagons.

Jennifer Holmes, Grade 4
Teacher: Esther Dickstein / Cathy Cuccio
Special Program for Individual Enrichment
Westcott School
Northbrook, Illinois

Purgatory

    I stumbled on one of the many divots in the hard-packed dirt road at the county fair. While catching my balance, I realized my temporary lack of muscle control had caused me to accidentally inhale through my already irritated nose. The fullness of the wreaking air from the enclosed barn filled my nostrils as my eyes squinted in distaste.

    The odor jogged my memory of the muggy insides of our family's mini-van and the lingering questions, "Why are we going here?" "I'm car sick." And my six-year-old sister's prime complaint, "Are we there yet?" This recollection only added to my utter confusion.

    I could not bear being trapped in this modern-day purgatory, but somehow the lady who dwelled in the ticket booth eating her granola bars and the twenty-year-old who worked in a portable hot dog stand had become tolerant of the smell or for some bizarre reason enjoyed it. This, I was not capable of.

    Hurrying my dad away from the cage of a 500-pound pig, I told him that there was but fifty feet of barn that separated me from fresh air. This thirteen-year-old was dedicated to escaping from the moist, heavy environment.

    Halfway through my pilgrimage to fresh air, I stepped in an ankle-deep puddle of murky water. I had already ruled out the possibility of getting "used to it," so my only option was to make a mad dash to the light at the end of the barn. Ecstatically, I scrambled into the radiance of clean air, much like walking through a tunnel to heaven.

    I raised my head in joy and inhaled the clean air—just as my dad signaled for me to enter the next barn.

Bryan Quinn, Grade 8
Teacher: Darlene Webb
Barrington Middle School
Barrington, Illinois

Infirmary

My stomach felt strange.
The nurse reminded me of a beach ball.
My legs stuck to the imitation leather chairs,
And my hair was stiff like straw
With chlorine and blood.

My arm was tired
From holding the bloody cloth to my head.
The strong smell of alcohol filled the room.
And I felt chilled,
Leaning against the pale green wall.

Hannah Kaufman, Grade 6
Teacher: Rhet Lickliter
Park Tudor Middle School
Indianapolis, Indiana

History of America

Christopher Columbus found this great old land;
He was the first white man to step on this sand.

The Pilgrims came a long, long way;
They came to find a free place to stay.

America would be free from England's rule;
The Colonists and English would fight a great duel.

The North and the South fought a great Civil War;
The North won the slaves' freedom and much more.

The Industrial Revolution caused a lot of pollution,
But it helped the evolution of our population.

World War I found Europe in distress;
We helped them out of the German's first mess.

In World War II, Germany was joined by Japan;
We helped stop them from killing civilized man.

During the Korean War, our country was all right,
But during the Vietnam War many refused to fight.

During the Civil Rights fight, Kennedy and King
    were killed;
So full of grief our country's heart was filled.

In the ten years of life that I have had,
Some things have been good and some things have
    been bad.

Even to this modern day,
History has a lot to say.

Jared Robertson, Grade 4
Teacher: Sandra Jones
Woodbrook Elementary School
Carmel, Indiana

Piano

Plink! Plunk! Plonk!
My fingers just won't work.
Plink! Plunk! Plonk!
There goes another wrong B-flat.
Plink! Plunk! Plonk!
Only twenty minutes left to go.
Plink! Plunk! Plonk!
Recital is not too far away.
Plink! Plunk! Plonk!
The ivory keys are really smudged.
Plink! Plunk! Plonk!
Keep my wrists out of the basement!
Plink! Plunk! Plonk!
Sit up straight.
Plink! Plunk! Plonk!
I think I've almost got it.
Plink! Plunk! Plonk!
Oh, drat! Beethoven, I am not.

Emily Paul, Grade 5
Teacher: Paula McGrew
Nishna Valley Community School
Hastings, Iowa

What's Under My Bed?

Have you ever thought what's under your bed?
Is it confusing in your head?
Maybe it's a monster, maybe it's scary,
Maybe it's a troll that's very, very hairy.
Maybe there're two monsters, or maybe three.
There might be some that want to eat me!

There might be people who come from Mars,
Because they don't like it up in the stars.
Is it my monkey that jumps in the air,
Or my doll, or my teddy bear?
It might be some little people who've come for a
    home,
They've come under my bed to look and roam.

At night when I rest my head,
I think of warlocks under my bed.
I bet they have some sisters, too,
Maybe one is named Lou.
I bet they're making magic potions.
They're using frogs and snakes for lotions.

I wonder what this is all about.
It's time to clean and I'll find out.
Maybe I should look under there.
Do you think I should? Do I dare?
Oh, I didn't have to worry at all,
It's just my junk and a great big dust ball!

Lindsay Lou Weilert, Grade 3
Sponsor / Librarian: Sister Romona Seidl
Blessed Sacrament School
Wichita, Kansas

America's Rock

In a faraway land and a long-ago time
A nation of miners mined.
They mined and dug all day and night,
But nothing did they find. . . .
Until the day they found a rock,
The most beautiful one they ever did see.
The size of a mountain it was, you know,
And such a rock could set them free.
The king was aware of this enormous stone,
And he was the only one who knew
That those who owned a piece of the rock
Could be granted freedom, too.
For the king alone was truly free,
(He owned the land; therefore, the stone),
But the miners soon discovered
What the king had wished unknown.
The people found what the rock could do,
The treasures it held in store.
So the miners won the rock;
They won it with a war.
After the rock was won from the king,
It was divided among all men.
Everyone with a piece of the rock
Discovered freedom then.
But some men had a bigger rock;
Thus, they knew more freedom, too.
And some had none at all.
Slavery was all they knew.
Soon the number of people grew,
And everyone's rock was divided again.
So even littler pieces of rock
Were given to the men.

I saw a small boy yesterday,
Covering his eyes as he wept.
I noticed a tiny bulge in his pocket
Where his rock was kept.
I stared at the child, his tear-streaked face,
And asked him why he cried.
He sniffled loudly and wiped his eyes
And finally replied:
"I only cry so hard because
My freedom rock is so small.
Such a little stone it is,
I haven't much freedom at all."
I stood there silent as he cried,
For I knew not what to say.
I clenched my own rock in my hand,
And started on my way.

Anna Van Cleave, Grade 8
Teacher: Stephanie Jacobson
Holy Trinity School
Lenexa, Kansas

He Always Wanted to Be Like...

Patrick was the middle-school class nerd. His only friends seemed to be the ants in his ant farm. He always wanted to be like Tim. He liked the way Tim walked, and he practiced walking like Tim every day and every night. Tim walked loosely and kind of half-strutted, half-floated down the middle-school hallways. Patrick wanted to be like Tim.

Tim was not particularly cool. In fact, he was known in middle school as the "geek." Tim always wanted to be like Alan. Using a tape recorder, Tim would practice making his voice deep and heavy like Alan's. Gosh, did Alan sound great!

Interestingly, Alan always wanted to be like Jason. Jason had great moves. Jason could stand, leaning against his locker, and spin a spiral notebook on the tip of his finger, like a professional basketball player showing off with a basketball. And he could bounce a soccerball between the gym wall and his foot for hours. Yes, Alan always wanted to be like Jason.

Jason liked his own moves all right, but he liked Robby's jokes better. He always wanted to be like Robby. "What happens when you throw a green rock in the Red Sea?" Jason would ask, and quickly follow with "It gets wet." When Robby told the same joke, kids would die laughing. But when Jason told it, they would just die.

Clearly, Robby was the funniest guy in middle school. He knew he wasn't very good with girls. That's why Robby always wanted to be like Billy. Robby liked the way Billy handled girls. But when Robby gave flowers to girls, the girls laughed. Girls laughed at Robby. They adored Billy.

Although Billy was good with the girls, the boys despised him. And Billy always wanted to be like Chris. Chris had the coolest clothes in school. Billy tried to dress like Chris. Billy's clothes made him look handsome but not "cool" like Chris.

Chris was nearly the most popular kid in school. But he wanted to be the most popular. He always wanted to be like Rick. Chris wanted Rick's popularity. He would do everything to be like Rick. Chris tried to walk like Rick, talk like Rick, dress like Rick, and act like Rick in the hallways.

Rick was the most popular boy in school. Everyone liked him. Teachers liked him. Even the vice principal (who didn't like anyone) liked Rick. The girls, the boys, the busdriver and the shop teacher all liked Rick. He was a model student. And everyone wanted to be just like him, and everyone pestered him to be their friend.

But Rick didn't particularly like all the attention. He liked peace and quiet. He liked doing things by himself. He liked sitting for hours and watching ants in an ant farm. And that's why he always wanted to be like the class nerd...Patrick. He always wanted to be like Patrick.

Chris Rupe, Grade 7
Teacher: Martin Gibbens
Robinson Middle School
Wichita, Kansas

The Future of America

The future of America
Depends upon me.
Reusing and recycling
Is the magic key.
Sorting out trash
Is the thing to do.
I can't wait for others
To do what I ought to.
I want to make America
How it should be.
I am the future;
The future is me.

Elizabeth Ainge Johnson, Grade 4
Teacher: Linda Leach
Good Shepherd School
Frankfort, Kentucky

The Sun

The glow of the sun
Comes from high up above.
Wearing his orange suit
And his bright yellow gloves.
His glowing toboggan
Made of bright red and gold
Shines like a beacon
As we all want to know.
"Why in the world,"
We shout to the sky,
"Why in the world
Are you dressed for snow?"
The sun sneezes,
"I've just got a cold."

Kim Wills, Grade 6
Teacher: Paul Medlar
Loyall Elementary School
Loyall, Kentucky

My Feelings Are Like a Rainbow

My feelings are like a rainbow.
They have different colors.

My feelings are red when I have to clean my
    room
And I don't want to—I feel mad.

My feelings are blue when I don't get along
With my friends—I feel sad.

My feelings are green when I see my friends
With their cats and dogs. I can't have one—
    I feel jealous.

My feelings are yellow when I am at school
With all my friends—I feel happy.

Veronica Saunders, Grade 1
Teacher: June Snyder
Cooper-Whiteside Primary School
Paducah, Kentucky

Stallions

The beasts rest in silence at the oasis.
Stallions! So calm, so solemn, so content.
Their heads bowing in the breeze—
Stallions! So magnificent, God's beasts, heaven-sent.
No other creature was there ever told,
To be so mysterious, so picturesque, so bold!

The beasts gallop briskly across the barren desert.
Stallions! So graceful, so poised, so free.
Their manes flowing in the wind—
Stallions! So exquisite, so beautiful, so holy.
Oh, how I love these creatures of the wild.
Their tempers flaring, never mild!

Nikki Boudreaux, Grade 8
Teacher: Shirley Newman
St. Thomas More School
Baton Rouge, Louisiana

The Barber's Chair

How I love to sit in the barber's chair
And have the barber cut my hair.
Snippity-snip, clickity-click.
The hair falls fast and thick.
He trims the sides, back, and top,
And then he finally stops.
Now I feel a buzz as he cuts behind my ears.
Afterwards, he lays down his shears.
He places them very neatly on the shelf,
Then I look in the mirror and hardly recognize
    myself.

Dennis Carheel, Grade 5
Teacher: Sharon Blake
Many Junior High School
Many, Louisiana

Tears

Little diamond droplets of feeling
That no robber would bother stealing.

Little drops of misery
Shed by both you and me.

No need to buy them in a store.
Hurt feelings will force your eyes to
Make more.

Tiny drops of frustration and pain
Which will surely cross your face again.

Gwen Jennings, Grade 8
Teacher: Heidi Campbell / Lynn Thompson
Harry M. Hurst Middle School
Destrehan, Louisiana

Masterpiece

The landscape of the United States is a masterpiece of great beauty and wonder. Its regions are neatly interwoven like pieces of a jigsaw puzzle.

Glaciers from long ago shaped the land as they carved out lakes, valleys, and plains. Pathways were formed for rushing rivers, strong streams, and thundering waterfalls.

Gently rolling hills grace the land as jagged mountain peaks pierce low-lying clouds in an effort to reach the sky.

Sandy beaches line the shores of the east coast while craggy walls of rock line the shores of the west coast.

Bands of forests zigzag across the mountains of the northeast and burst into brilliant colors with the coming of fall.

The rugged mountains of the west are rocky and bare as they tower above the land. The lower slopes are covered with evergreens while the white snowcapped peaks glisten in the sun. Above the timberline where trees cannot grow live bighorn sheep, deer, and mountain lions.

In between the mountain ranges are miles of deserts, canyons, and wide open space.

Dry, grassy ranges stretch out endlessly under the sun's rays while herds of cattle lazily graze.

The landscape of the United States is a mosaic of many different shapes, forms, and colors. It is truly a masterpiece.

Matthew Kuzio, Grade 4
Teacher: J. Christine Paulsell
Mandeville Middle School
Mandeville, Louisiana

How They All Belong Together

How the petals of a daisy all gather to make one—
How the children of the summer join together to
    have fun—
How the raindrops from the sky all fall and form a
    puddle—
How the teenagers at school all become one large
    huddle—
How the sweet old ladies in the home all chat over
    tea—
How they all belong together
Is how I'd like to be.

Erika Laughlin, Grade 8
Teacher: Sharon Wood
Mandeville Junior High School
Mandeville, Louisiana

The Boy Who Loved Pancakes

Once upon a time there was a little boy named Rance who loved pancakes. Pancakes were his most favorite food in the world.

Every night when Rance's mom would tuck him into bed, he would ask, "Can we have pancakes for breakfast?"

She would smile and say, "Yes."

Soon Rance was fast asleep, dreaming about pancakes. Suddenly, he was in pancake land! It was unbelievable! There were mountains and mountains of pancakes, rivers and rivers of syrup with butterfalls of butter.

Rance was so happy to be in pancake land that the first thing he did was run to the river and taste the sweet syrup. It tasted so delicious that he just wanted to eat a great big stack of pancakes. There was only one problem; the pancakes were too big!

Rance looked around. There had to be a small pancake mountain somewhere in pancake land. He decided to go searching along the river. He had an idea! He would use one of the big pancakes as a raft to float down the river.

All of a sudden the river started flowing faster and faster. He could not stop! He just closed his eyes and swoosh, down he went over a butterfall.

When he opened his eyes, he could hardly believe what he saw. Right in front of him were the most delicious breakfast foods. There were sausage links, bowls full of grits, giant biscuits with jelly, and lots and lots of orange juice.

Seeing all of that food made him even more hungry. Rance got off of the raft and quickly found himself a small pancake mountain. It was just the right size to eat.

Rance was about to take a bite when he felt a nudge to his shoulder. In a voice far away, his mom called, "Rance, it's time to wake up."

Rance was a little sad to wake up from his dream, but his sadness did not last long. Waiting for him at the breakfast table was a stack of pancakes just his size.

Kristy Lasseigne, Grade 2
Teacher: Elaine Knight
Galliano Elementary School
Galliano, Louisiana

Friends Stick Together

Once upon a time there lived a small kitten. Her name was Rosie. One day her mom said, "Rosie, dear, it is your first day of school."

Slowly, Rosie pulled down the covers. She got dressed and brushed her teeth and went downstairs to eat breakfast. She put on her coat and said goodbye to her mom and dad.

She waited for the bus outside her house. When the bus came, she looked back at her mom and dad. They smiled back at her.

She climbed up into the big yellow bus. The bus was very noisy. Sitting across from her was a little kitten just like her. The kitten looked sad.

Just then the bus stopped in front of the school. Rosie got off the bus and went inside. She met her teacher in the hall. She said, "Rosie, would you like me to show you where your coat hanger is?"

Inside the room, there were kids playing with blocks and kids reading. Her teacher showed her her hook.

Then her teacher led Rosie over to the corner. There was the same little kitten that looked so sad on the bus. Her teacher said, "This is Lily. I'm sure you'll be best friends." She left them and went to talk to some other girls.

Just then the bell rang. They sat down at their seats. They sang, "I've Been Working on the Railroad." They rested on the rug. The teacher read them a story. The two girls giggled when the teacher messed up.

Then they had music. They looked at a book together and ate a snack. Rosie shared her crackers with Lily.

After school, Mom said to her, "How was your day at school?"

Rosie said, "I found out that friends always stick together."

Caitlin Fitzgerald, Grade 1
Teacher: Beth Guiseley
Rockport Elementary School
Rockport, Maine

The Sea

It tempted; it beckoned; it called to me,
To that part of my soul I could not suppress.
It lodged deep within my heart, I confess,
The wildness, the glory, of the sea.

It was Fate's decree—one I could not ignore.

My heart dwelled not within the land
With its meadows and flowers and trees,
But with the salt in the air, in the wind,
    in the breeze,
And the memory of seashells upon the sand.

My heart belonged to me no more.

It belonged to the sea, whose every whim
Put the mortal at the mercy of the sea god's fancy,
(Or maybe a sea witch's necromancy),
But dangers do not make our spirits dim.

What makes us love the ocean so?

The sea has beauty unsurpassed:
The waves which swell and ebb from the shore;
The shore that grows farther till we see it no more,
And we know that our destiny's die has been cast.

The sea owns us; it makes our lifeblood flow.

The depths of the sea intrigue me much;
Do the ocean's fathoms reach no end?
And the stars, at night they're my only friends
That sometimes seem close enough to touch.

And its color, which changes from green to blue.

The storm clouds come closer, absorbing the azure
Of the sky. In our breasts, there is a cold, stark fear
That we will not live to see the sun as dawn grows
    near,
But we do not regret succumbing to the ocean's
    lure,

Though sometimes deaths are many and survivors
    few.

The lightning, it flashes, blinding and bright.
The thunder reverberates within my head.
Rain plasters my hair to my skull; but I dread
The claws of death that I cannot fight.

But I am a seaman, so I must try.

We weather the storm, and are safe once again.
As we toil, we sing a sailor's tune.
And at night, beneath the silver rays of the moon,
We give thanks to the gods for sparing us men.

I dream sometimes of a life that has passed me by.

The life of a husband, or father, or both.
I will leave no sons, and will have no real home
But this ship and the ocean I will endlessly roam.
But I could not support a family to feed and clothe.

For my soul would be forever searching and
    yearning.

For the sun upon the crest of a wave;
The wind in sails and cradle-like swaying;
With the music of mermaids, laughing and playing;
And the ocean's perils, I would fearlessly brave.

For the sea keeps my life's fire burning.

One day, the ocean's secrets will be revealed to
    me.
The waves whisper a melody only I understand.
The sea croons to me a lullaby.
Above me the squawking sea gulls fly,
But they know not of the sea's wonders,
    of why it's so grand,

Why its sacred, pagan loveliness sets caged spirits
    free.

But I love the sea, hence I know
Of why the waves curl and the biting winds blow.
And when death comes, I'll let it capture me,
For I have known the untamed beauty of the sea.

I have known the sea.

Clarissa Martinez, Grade 8
Teacher: Mary Jane McCall
Holton-Arms School
Bethesda, Maryland

The Candle

"When the candle has burned to a stump," he told me, "those nasty intentions to bully people or to sass your teachers will never return to your mind again. Every time you do a good deed, light your candle and slowly count to ten. If you do a good deed every day, then in thirty days the candle will be used up." I grabbed the tall, skinny candle and ran off. I admit that I was a nasty little brute, but I meant well and would do almost anything to become nice.

I ran home and stumbled in through the door. Panting for breath I flopped on my bed, put the candle on my night table, and fell asleep.

In the morning I couldn't find my candle, but there was a strange voice inside me. It came from the depth of my stomach and mingled up to my heart, where it would say things like, "Don't hit your brother!" or "Don't muss the living room!" I would ALWAYS obey the voice's commands. Once the voice even told me to play with my brother, and I actually did! It wasn't like me, and the little pest noticed it and felt my forehead.

About four weeks passed, and the voice continued to coach me. I had given up on looking for my candle. "I don't need it anymore," I told myself. After all, I had improved tremendously without it.

"Do the dishes!" the voice told me. I did. "Pat your brother!" I did. "Mow the lawn!" I did. "Clean your room!" As usual, I obeyed.

I organized my trinkets, folded my clothes. Then I picked up my crayons. I sorted them by color. First red, then blue, then...my candle! It must have fallen from my night table and gotten in with my crayons. Funny, though. It was only a stump.

Emily Pulfer-Terino, Grade 5
Teacher: JoAnn Callaghan
Mount Everett Regional School
Sheffield, Massachusetts

Me

When I look in the mirror,
Who do I see?
A lot of hair, two eyes, and a nose.
But there's something else,
Something under the skin,
That is me.

That something comes out of me
In different ways.
It can be seen easily in my writing.
It shows in my dancing and soccer
And in the way I dress.

I like my soft long hair and blue eyes,
But I hate the tear that I see too often,
And the missing key for math.
I hate the metal that covers
My buck teeth at night.

But all that makes me
Who I am,
And my something is Alison,
And nobody has my something.

Alison Turnbull, Grade 4
Teacher: Carol St. John
Doyon School
Ipswich, Massachusetts

That Cold Winter Day

It has been almost a year since my grandpa died. As the Christmas season is coming, I am starting to think what it will be like to spend Christmas without him. My mind also drifts back to the day he died.

The day was January fifth. I was at forensics practice after school. My mom was also helping out at the practice because the first meet was a week away and the coaches needed all the help that they could get to prepare for it. I had just finished reading my piece when my mom came bursting through the door. She told me to grab my books because we were leaving. I immediately knew what happened.

As we raced to my grandma's house in our car, I really had to fight to keep from breaking out in tears.

When we got there my mom and sister rushed into my grandpa's room, but I did not. It was too hard to accept that he was gone now, and I knew that if I saw him it would only make it harder. As I stood crying in the living room, my grandma and aunt tried to comfort me, but it didn't help much. I wasn't crying so much because of sadness, but just because the thought of him not being there came as such a shock that I didn't know what to feel.

One by one the rest of the people close to my grandpa came to see him.

When my dad came to see my grandpa, I finally found the courage to go into his room. He looked so peaceful. He had been sick with cancer for many years. I knew that it made him sad that he couldn't do as many things as he did before, although he never admitted it. Now it was all over.

As I was saying goodbye to my grandpa with the rest of my relatives, the paramedics came. While they were putting him on the stretcher and strapping him down, I reached out to touch his hand. It was cold and fleshy. That is when the feeling hit me. My grandpa was dead and these people were here to take him away. I wanted to yell for them to stop, to leave him here so that I could see him again. I wanted it all to be a dream. I wanted my grandpa back. They loaded my grandpa into the ambulance like he was any old person, but in my heart I knew he wasn't. He was my grandpa.

On that cold winter day when my grandpa died...he took a piece of my heart with him.

Joe Piech, Grade 7
Teacher: Kay O'Neill
St. Paul School
Grosse Pointe Farms, Michigan

Seasons

Spring

A cheerful weeping willow swayed peacefully over a gold-green lake encrusted in bobbing rubies. Gentle waves rolled softly across the lake's top, rearranging the rubies' intricate patterns. The weeping willow's soft strings of spring-green were blown softly upward and dripped diamond-like drops of water into the lake as though it were weeping. Red and pink clouds spanned the sky. A wind blew softly. Raindrops began to fall erratically, then more frequently. Split! Splat! Split! Splat! A cool wind rumpled the lake's surface violently. At last the rain was falling steadily. The first spring rain!

Summer

A droopy weeping willow with velvet strings of leaves bent heavily over a still brown-green lake. It was motionless, like everything else on the humid, heavy day. A flash of heat lightning brightened the hazy, heavy, sunless sky. A grumpy brown bullfrog plopped carelessly into the murky water. The weeping willow's vine-like branches rested their tips in the cool lake as though they were sipping its water. The faint sound of children laughing was the only sound to be heard. A flash of lightning streaked across the sky, though this time it was followed by a roar of thunder that sounded like an old, meek man groaning in pain. Another blinding flash of lightning shot across the sky. It was quickly followed by a roar of thunder that sounded like a grumpy old man growling madly. Then big raindrops began to fall, causing little explosions in the dust. Then it came down in sheets. The first summer storm!

Fall

A lonely weeping willow stood sadly above a still silver-gray lake. The willow's yellowing strings of leaves brushed the pulsing surface as though it were made of its own tears. A cold harsh wind blew across the field at the north like a cold knife. It scattered an assortment of yellow, red, orange, and brown leaves. It upset piles of leaves, tallies of the raking that had taken place that morning. The sky dimmed. Gray and fluorescent pink clouds cloaked the gray sky. The deathly silence told the coming of a storm. The world was still, waiting. Then it came. Cold pellets of rain. The first autumn storm!

Winter

A leafless weeping willow decorated in red satin bows bent cheerfully over an ice-skating rink, slick and polished. The delectable smell of hot chocolate faded with the laughter of the retired skaters that were now mere dots in the distance. Big fluffy snowflakes began to fall, their designs as intricate as the richest lace. Fluffy gray clouds hid a gray sky. Strong ice-like winds were picking up from the north. There would soon be a blizzard. A stillness filled the icy air. A violent gust of wind followed. The snow was a thick mist. The first winter storm!

Kristin Poling, Grade 4
Teacher: Nancy Stefan
Field Elementary School
Minneapolis, Minnesota

Waterfall

A waterfall is like silver beads
Tumbling off rocks, and if you
Watch long enough you will wonder
Where it leads and what you'll
Find if you follow.

Its cool breeze is like a small
Hand brushing by your cheek.
You want it to come back and
Touch you again.

Mist floats in the air everywhere—
Along the river below,
Above the bridge—
Hugging the treetops.

Kristina Beyer, Grade 6
Teacher: Elizabeth Aase
Mann Elementary School
St. Paul, Minnesota

School

School has changed much through the years,
Starting with people like pioneers.
But they weren't as lucky as we are today;
They did things the old-fashioned way.
All the classes were stuck in one room,
Probably crowded, you would naturally
    assume.
At that time, the children weren't free.
They had not one bit of liberty.
But now things aren't like the colonial days;
Things differ in many, many ways.
We have light, electricity;
One class, one room—not crowded, you see.
I sometimes want to live back then,
But Pilgrims might tell me to think again.

Amber Fikes, Grade 5
Teacher: Claudia Hopkins
Church Street School
Tupelo, Mississippi

Leaf Ballet

"Autumn has come!
Autumn has come!"
The king tree announced.
All of us leaves got ready
For the annual ballet.
We had practiced in the wind
Since spring.
We dressed in our colorful costumes.
One by one we danced;
Two by two we pranced;
Three by three,
Four by four,
Five by five,
Constantly growing in numbers,
We flitted and fluttered
To the ground.
Soon the tree cried.
We all said, "Goodbye!"
The dance was over.
Autumn was over.
Our lives would soon be over.

Lynn Gaither, Grade 7
Teacher: Marcia Johnson
Phelps Center for Gifted
Springfield, Missouri

She Doesn't Look a Hundred

"Mom," I said, "when will the fireworks start?"
"When it gets dark," she replied.

My parents and I sat by the harbor in the slowly darkening twilight, looking out on the water that reflected the bright city lights. I stared at the Statue of Liberty standing straight and proud in all her glory. Once, she had gleamed golden in the sunlight, but time had taken its toll. The copper was green now, and the beautiful lady had crumbled. For the past year she had been surrounded by a hideous scaffold with men swarming over it, preparing her for her 100th birthday.

Several times my family and I had ridden a ferry boat that passed Liberty Island. I could see the outline of the statue and the features of her face. I had seen the scaffolding and sometimes minute, black dots moving about on it. I raced through time and imagined the moment when they would take down the ugly structure.

Now the scaffold had been taken down, and the statue was lovely again. A century ago the United States received her as a gift from France. It is said that Frederic Auguste Bartholdi, her sculptor, modeled her to look like his mother.

It all seemed so long ago. It is almost impossible for a six-year-old to comprehend 100 years. All that mattered was the present, July 4, 1986.

Kaboom! The fireworks had started. I looked up and saw a red ball of fire fade away. A blue flower-like shape rose through the air behind the Statue of Liberty to replace it. It was followed, a moment later, by a deafening thunderclap. I put my hands over my ears. Before this one had completely vanished, a green one appeared, then orange, yellow, purple, blue, green, and red in rapid succession, making terrific popping and booming noises.

Even now, nearly five years later, I can close my eyes and relive it all—the fireworks, how Dad bought some Statue of Liberty T-shirts, the walk home. As I lay in bed that night, I thought, "She really doesn't look like she's 100." Then I dropped off to sleep, knowing I would remember that day forever.

Amanda Williams, Grade 6
Teacher: Marilyn Morrison
Wydown Middle School
Clayton, Missouri

How the Rainbow Trout Got Its Rainbow

Once the rainbow trout was only an ugly gray trout. This was back in the days when rainbows touched the earth at both ends and each end had a pot of gold. Not one pot was bigger than another.

The otter loved to eat fish, and the trout was so camouflaged, he was hard to catch. The otter hated this. The trout didn't like his appearance either. He wanted a bright colorful coat like his cousin the salmon. The otter knew this, so he tried to think of a way to get the fish brighter and easier to catch.

After a while he thought of a plan. He called the trout over to his house for tea. As they were talking, the otter told the trout that he thought there was a way to get him a new coat. After the otter had explained part of his plan, the trout agreed. Just then it started raining.

"We won't have to wait very long now," said the trout. Soon it stopped raining. A brilliant rainbow appeared in the east.

"Well, come on," said the otter. "This is what we were waiting for." They headed for the nearest end of the rainbow.

When they got there, they found a pot of gold. The otter said, "You can have this pot. I will take the other one."

Then the fish took a pair of scissors and climbed a tree right by the rainbow. He cut off as much of the rainbow as he could. They went to the other end of the rainbow. The otter took the second pot of gold and gave the fish some scissors and a ladder. "Now you climb up and cut off some more of the rainbow while I hold the ladder," he said to the trout.

The fish did as the otter told him. Then they went home. All that night the fish sewed the pieces of rainbow into a very well-fitting suit. The next day he went to show the otter.

The otter said, "Those are fine clothes. Why don't you take the scraps and make some more for your friends. I don't need one myself." So the trout did.

This was what the otter's plan had been. He had planned to make all the gray fish brightly colored. When he did they would be easier to see and catch.

But it didn't quite work the way he had planned, because the trout moved fast and looked like rays of sunlight on the water. And the trout were no easier to catch than before.

Seth Bloom, Grade 3
Teacher: Pat Tibbs
Corvallis Primary School
Corvallis, Montana

Chapter 1

Once upon a time, there was a little boy who loved school. When he was in the first grade, he loved school because his teacher was very affectionate. She loved the children, even the ones who were naughty. She hugged them and kissed them and gave them lots of warm fuzzies. She was young and gorgeous.

When the year was over, he felt very glum and gloomy. On the last day of school, he was quiet and sad inside. When the time came to say goodbye, he cried like he had never cried before. The teacher cried, too, because she loved the little boy. He went out the door but couldn't leave. He stayed by the door, waiting until everyone left. Then the teacher and the boy talked and hugged, and then the boy slowly walked out of the school with his head down.

That summer, the boy moved far away across the state to a big city. He worried about being kidnapped and going to a new school. He heard strange noises at night in his new house and they scared him, too.

The first day of school was hard, at least the first ten minutes were. When he walked into the building he felt as if he had shrunk and no one could see him. He was thankful to have his mother beside him. They walked into the classroom. The teacher was talking to one of the other mothers. The little boy kissed his mother goodbye, and his mother said, "Good luck."

The teacher was serious but nice. Lunch was similar to lunch at the old school, but at this school all the boys sat at the same table and all the girls sat at a different one. The day went quickly and it was time to say goodbye, but her hug wasn't the same. He felt like he was hugging a rock.

That day, when he went home, his mother asked if he had a nice day. He said, "It was okay, I guess." He went up to his room, shut his door, got out a picture of his old teacher, and cried.

David Goeschel, Grade 3
Teacher: Sharon Sorich
Loveland Elementary School
Omaha, Nebraska

I Battle Myself

*Dedicated to all those who care to fight
for our nation.*

The crimson heat but warms my heart,
The hypnotic beat of teardrops start.
So forth another day I live,
To find a different way to give.
"Now I lay me down to sleep,
I pray my soul the Lord shall keep,"
And if I wake and don't retreat,
Another quest and friend I'll meet.
My loved ones cry, my comrades die,
My biggest task to face is I.
The larger the leap, the bigger the weep,
At least the fall I take isn't steep.
I serve my realm, and keep it true,
The battle I win is all for you.
My price is small, my deed is done,
I won't show pride until I've won.

Kirby Conn, Grade 6
Teacher: Mike McDonald
Las Vegas Day School
Las Vegas, Nevada

America My Country

America my country,
A nation proud and free,

From the mountains to the valleys,
How beautiful to me.

America my country,
Land of many races,

From brave men like Columbus,
Of many different places.

America my country,
Sweet land of liberty,

From Washington and Lincoln,
To Jefferson and Lee.

America my country,
You stand for strength and peace.

For the help you give to others,
My love will never cease.

America my country,
A nation proud and free,

From the mountains to the valleys,
How beautiful to me!

Matthew T. Gorski, Grade 5
Teacher: Sandra Ouellet
Hampstead Middle School
Hampstead, New Hampshire

Life in America

Life is about almost anything,
From electric keyboards to bells that ring.
But the thing I like best about life today
Is that I can say what I want to say.
Freedom is what I'm talking about.
I have freedom to yell and freedom to shout.
I have freedom of speech, I have freedom of choice.
I don't have to listen to a king raise his voice.
There's lots of freedom everywhere.
There's enough freedom for everyone to share.

Justin Hatch, Grade 3
Teacher: Bruce Hatch
Grant M. Bowler Elementary School
Logandale, Nevada

The Fox and the Goat

One day a fox fell into a well. He had wanted to get a drink, but when he did, he tumbled into the well, and he couldn't get out. Try as he would, he simply could not get himself out.

"I must get out of here," thought the fox. As the fox was thinking about what to do next, a goat came by, looking for some water.

"Friend Fox," called the goat as he spied the fox down in the well, "how do you find the water down there?"

The fox looked up at the goat and replied, "It's as clear as any water can be! You would do well to come down here in order to see and enjoy the water for yourself."

"Let me think," the goat said. He thought about this idea for a minute and then decided, "That I will do," as he jumped excitedly down into the well.

As the goat put his head down to try to drink the water, the fox jumped up on his back, and with one more jump he was out of the well. "I'm glad that's over," Fox said, talking to himself.

When the goat saw what the fox had done, he was surprised and angry. "Just a minute, you trickster," called the goat. "How am I going to get out of here?" The fox could not hold his laughter. "You should have thought of that before you jumped down," he mocked. "Next time, look before you leap!" And then the fox went on his happy way singing.

Moral: Don't trust anyone who:

- makes strange suggestions.
- talks to you from the bottom of a well.
- has a reputation for being sneaky.

And always look before you leap.

Angel Calderon, Grade 7
Teacher: Michelle Postema
The Mustard Seed School
Hoboken, New Jersey

Eternity

A last gasping breath for life;
The end is near.
One falls,
Then another,
Until there is nothing but dancing colors of death.
The challenger of the dying laughs.
He knows he shall win,
For the cycle must turn.

Those days are now forgotten.
The sheet of gleam settles.
A howling wind of victory is released.
The land is calm,
Peaceful.

The loser of the battle has not forgotten;
He shall seek revenge.
With his newly gathered strength he appears.
Slowly the blanket dissolves.
The victor has now lost to the loser.
He gives in without a struggle,
For unlike summer, winter knows the path of eternity
Cannot be changed.

Sonali Das, Grade 7
Teacher: Susan Sorkenn
Eric S. Smith School
Ramsey, New Jersey

The Future Bridge

As Lydia walked down the aisle, she felt nervous.
She had known that she would, but she wasn't
prepared. Her heart was pounding so hard that her
chest began to hurt. She had waited twelve years for
this day, and now it was here.

Lydia wanted to go back in time, she wanted to
run and hide. As music throbbed in her ears, she
walked on, realizing that this moment was her bridge
to adulthood. The diploma was the ticket to the rest
of her life!

Tosha Samuels, Grade 7
Teacher: Rita Schlom
Grice Middle School
Trenton, New Jersey

The Life of Vincent James Fusaro

Once in Cosenza, Italy, in 1878, a man named
Vincent James Fusaro was born. Vincent came from
a poor family. His father, Vincent, was a grocer. His
mother, Marietta, was a housewife.

His parents wanted Vincent to have a better life.
So at the age of 14, Vincent, by himself, left Naples,
Italy, for America. Every night on the ship, the men
slept in a different room from the women.
Everybody slept on bunks. Many, many people got
sick. Some people died. Some babies were born on
the ship. There were doctors aboard. Meals were in
a dining room. The trip took ten days. Nothing
about the boat was luxurious. Most of the boats
were either tankers or cargo ships.

Vincent had heard from others that America was a
place where there were many opportunities. It was
easier to find houses, jobs, and, best of all, freedom.
Vincent was used to working hard and was willing
to work as much as needed for good money.

Finally, the boat docked in Ellis Island, New York.
It was scary for Vincent to be in a new country. No
job, no home, and not knowing a word of English.
When he got to the dock, he went to a consulate to
register as a citizen. He had to get a vaccination shot
and a physical. They also inspected his belongings.

Then he moved to Old Forge, Pennsylvania, to
live with friends. He became a coal miner, but a
couple of years later, he decided that his life was
not good enough for him. So he moved to Nutley,
New Jersey, with other friends. He went to night
school and learned to read, write, and speak the
English language.

In those days, families arranged marriages for their
children. When he was twenty-two, he was matched
up to marry Christina Gaccione. Her parents agreed
for Christina to marry Vincent because he was
starting a new life in America.

He learned to be a shoemaker. He was taught to
make and repair shoes. At first he went to other
people's houses to repair their shoes. Later he was
able to open his own shop. His business grew, and
he became a well-respected man in his community.

They had a family of seven children: Anthony,
Frank, Marietta, Julia, Rosie, James, and Jennie. His
children were able to go to school and get an
education. He taught his sons how to repair and
make shoes. He showed them a much better life
than they would have had in Italy. He lived in the
same house until he died in 1969.

Vincent James Fusaro was my great-great-
grandfather. His daughter, Julia, married Frank
Gabriel. They are my great-grandparents. Vincent
Fusaro's courage to start a new life in America has
given me the many opportunities that I have today.

Richard McKelvey, Grade 4
Teacher: Patricia Bishop
Washington Street School
Toms River, New Jersey

Going West

First one,
Then a few,
Then a trickle,
Then a stream,
Finally a river
Rushing,
Gushing,
Following fortune,
Going west.

Afraid of
Indians,
Tomahawks,
The coyote's cry,
Howling,
Growling,
Chilling,
But still
Following fortune,
Going west.

Then
The call of gold,
The river
Becomes a sea.
The call to battle,
The Indians
Rise and fight.
Danger increases,
Scalped settlers
But more
Following fortune,
Going west.

The Indians
Put down.
Free land!

The sea
Becomes an
Ocean.
Hardship,
Poor crops,
The land
Is full.
The ocean becomes a
Sea becomes a
River becomes a
Stream becomes a
Trickle,
But still
Following fortune,
Going West.

Years pass,
Cities grow,
But
The trickle
Is still
There,
And the
Drama, the
Dreams lost
And found,
Riches gained,
Riches lost,
An era gone.
Only the
Marks remain
Of following fortune,
Going west.

Elizabeth Weissel, Grade 6
Teacher: Denise Gormley
Brookside School
Allendale, New Jersey

Eight-Second Ride

You're down in the chute, your hands are all sweaty,
Warm up your rope, everything is ready.
Tighten your hat,
Scoot up real slow,
And with a nod of your head, you're rearing to go.
He spins and kicks with all of his might.
An eight-second ride is what this cowboy wants
    tonight.
The crowd goes wild as he hits the ground.
He tips his hat and looks around.
The world goes silent as the announcer sounds.
An eighty-five is called as he receives the crown!
He wears a buckle proud instead of a frown.
The eight-second ride is the talk of the town.
A hero he is as this rodeo winds down.
And at the end of the night,
He's won with all of his might,
It's on to the next town and rodeo fight.

Ryan Grandi, Grade 7
Teacher: Hildegard Adams
Taylor Middle School
Albuquerque, New Mexico

A Capital Story

"I told you, you can fly!" insisted the strange little
    man, whose name was Bismarck. He had fuzzy
    hair and a frizzy beard.
"But that isn't possible," Pierre argued. He kicked
    nervously at a little rock.
"Nothing is impossible," said Bismarck.
"But I'm *positive* nobody can fly."
"You can—if you try," Bismarck said.
Pierre took a big breath. He thought to himself,
    Paris is a long way from Washington, D.C., but
    that's how far I'll have to fly if I ever want to be
    home again.
"I'll give you my magic blessing," said Bismarck.
    His dark eyes twinkled, and he began to chant a
    song: "Tail of lizard, ice of blizzard, sizzle and
    make Pierre fly."
Bismarck sure was impressing Pierre. Maybe it
    wasn't impossible to fly.
"Stand aside!" Pierre warned. He closed his eyes
    and started to move and . . .

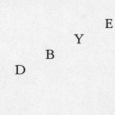

"G O O D B Y E !"

The Concorde took to the sky.

Michael Smith, Grade 3
Teacher: Polly Tausch
S.Y. Jackson School
Albuquerque, New Mexico

A Wish for the World

The gunshots have all faded
And the tanks all roll away
And they say the war is over
But I know it's here to stay.
The feelings that have built up
During the bitter fight
I know will stay with people
Throughout the day and night.
I hope that in the future
The sickness known as hate
Can be stopped from spreading
Before it gets too late.
I hope that in the future
That we make up our minds
To stop the war and fighting
And bring peace to humankind.

Laura Donnelly, Grade 6
Teacher: Kathy B. Fleischman
Amherst Middle School
Snyder, New York

The Night I Had the Most Fun

As I was walking down the street
One dark and stormy night,
I saw some strange shapes
That happened to give me a fright.
At the end of my journey,
Much to my surprise,
I was looking right into
A 399-pound bear's eyes!
As I tried to run
I stepped on his toes,
And he lifted me
Right up by my nose.
I was so scared
My face turned red,
Thinking I would probably
End up dead.
Then he roared a mighty roar.
You might think it absurd,
But at that very moment
You'll never guess what I heard.
The bear sang like Sinatra,
He sang like no other,
But then I was shaken
By the hand of my mother.
It had all been a dream,
But a very realistic one.
Surely that was the night
I had the most fun.

Jacqueline Ganz, Grade 5
Teacher: Linda Greenfield
Vanderbilt Elementary School
Dix Hills, New York

My Great Adventure

One of the best things in America is its amusement parks. Of course, that's from the perspective of an eleven-year-old boy, which is what I am. All rides are fun, but roller coasters are what I love best. The speed, the ups, the downs, the upside-downs are what make roller rides my favorite—or at least that's what I thought.

We were on our way to Great Adventure Amusement Park in New Jersey when my friend, Adam, asked if I was going on the Great American Scream Machine. I said I wasn't sure. But, in my heart, I knew I couldn't face that ride. The 173-foot-high, seven-loop, sixty-eight-mile-per-hour roller coaster made my stomach do flips just thinking about it. And thinking about it is what I'd been doing for weeks.

When Adam saw the ride, he commented on how scary it looked, but he still wanted to go on it. Now, I didn't know what to do. We'd gone on most of the rides when my dad said we'd better go on the Scream Machine before it got too late. I was hoping the park would close before we got on, because I was really scared. I was more than scared; I was terrified. But a boy's got to do what a boy's got to do, especially if his best friend is going to call him a chicken. So we got in line.

As we were waiting, I prayed for some kind of setback, anything that would give me time to get out of this mess. My prayers worked. We were in the middle of the line when the roller coaster stopped running. "Mom must be worried, don't you think? Maybe we better go back," I said. It was a good try, but Adam and my dad didn't buy it. They insisted on waiting until the ride was working again. About five minutes later, it started rolling.

I sat down in the car and chills ran through my body. I hoped a priest would come to give me my last rites. I had every reason to believe I wouldn't survive this. When the cars started moving, I knew my fate was sealed.

We reached the top, and my dad yelled, "This is a nasty drop," and we plunged into the darkness of the night. We neared the first loop, and I nearly wet my pants. I didn't like the idea of going upside-down, but, as I thought this, we were halfway through the loop. When we came upright again, I realized I was actually having a pretty good time. This roller coaster was fantastic! Of course, it went so fast that, by the time I figured this out, it was over. I did it!

All the way home we talked about the Great American Scream Machine. Adam said he heard about a 196-foot-high roller coaster in Ohio. Maybe. . . .

Kevin Kuffner, Grade 6
Teacher: Daniel Domingo
Public School 114Q
Belle Harbor, New York

Peace

The Peace
Old, yet unused
Sits and waits
Quietly
Undying.

Sam Cone, Grade 4
Teacher: Mary Claiborne
Wiley Acceleration and Enrichment Center
Greensboro, North Carolina

The Little Rose Tree

Every rose on the little tree
    is making a different face at me.
Some look surprised when I go by;
    others droop as if they were shy.
These two here whose heads together press
    tell secrets I could never guess.
Some have their heads thrown back to sing
    and all the buds are listening.
I wonder if the gardener knows,
    or if he calls each just a rose?

Jamie Krause, Grade 8
Teacher: Mary Combs
Cool Spring Elementary School
Cleveland, North Carolina

The Best Christmas

Do you think of Christmas as a day to amass presents? I did too, until one Christmas several years ago. My brother was hoping for a new bicycle. Since I didn't have enough money to get him one, I asked my mother if we could get his old one fixed.

So my mother drove me over to the bike shop in Waynesville. We walked into a gray stone building, past rows of dismantled bicycles, into a cold little room. An old man was sitting in a corner near a greasy potbelly stove. We told him about our bike's problem, and he smiled and said it would be as good as new by Christmas. Later we picked it up on December 23. Now, however, I started thinking how awful it must be for that old man to stay in that cold, dark building. We went to an adjacent drugstore for some aspirin and asked the owner about the man next door. The man, it seemed, lived alone and slept on a small rollaway bed in the store. He was crippled with arthritis and had one son nearby who ignored him. Then we asked where the old man would be staying for Christmas. "He'll be inside the shop as he always is," was the reply. We bought our aspirin and left, but now I was really worried about the old man.

Our family always has a big Christmas with ten children to celebrate. Our grandmothers vie over giving us the best presents, and later we go to my father's godfather's house to have roast pig. This year our family was going to play our instruments for the guests. With two trumpets, two French horns, a trombone, and my bassoon, we have quite a band. We were going to play several Christmas carols. We had to pack our van with all the instruments, music stands, and presents.

I begged to take yet another thing—a turkey dinner from the refrigerator. "For what?" asked my parents. Well, we would be going right past the bike shop in Waynesville. What was the poor old man doing on such a cold Christmas? So I took the turkey dinner and held it on my lap until Waynesville. We went into the cold, damp building where the old man sat on his bed wrapped in a thin woolen blanket. I gave him the dinner, we played a few Christmas carols and left. Even though the old man didn't say much, I could see we made his day happier. I was certainly happier.

Later in January we went to Waynesville again, but the store seemed to be empty. Again we asked the druggist next door, who told us the man had died. I fought back my tears. Now several years have gone by, but when I pass that way, especially around Christmas time, I think of the old man and the dinner we brought him, and I must confess that I think his last Christmas may have been one of his best. It certainly was one of mine.

Alexandra Gilman, Grade 8
Teacher: Carolyn A. Wike
Camp Laboratory School
Cullowhee, North Carolina

Blazet and Dapple

There were once two horses. One, which was a palomino, had the name of Blazet. Dapple, Blazet's friend, was gray and white. They were often paired together to haul meat in the daytime or lead cabs at night. This is a story about them as cab horses one September night in 1878.

"Cab!" screamed a lady. Dan, Blazet's and Dapple's owner, reined back his horses. "Thank you so much, sir," said the lady with a kind pat to Dapple and Blazet. "To Mr. James Manson's, please."

When they arrived at their destination, Dapple and Blazet were exhausted. Dan told the lady the cab fee. It had been a long, tiring day for Dan, and he was eager to get home.

"The party will only last until 10:00, so wait for me," said the woman.

"But, Ma'am, I'm so tired and so are my horses. I just won't be able to stay," said Dan.

"Sir, I refuse to pay you until after the party, when you've returned me safely home!"

"Yes, Ma'am."

Dan, Blazet, and Dapple had been waiting for a while when the clouds started turning gray. Then the heavy rain came. The other cab horses started to get nervous from the storm. The horses were so hard to control that the other cab drivers decided to leave— but not Dan. He knew his horses could withstand the cold rain and loud thunder.

It was nearly midnight when Miss Emiline Bultema finally appeared at the door with six of her friends. She was laughing and said to Dan, "We need a cab and horses that can carry seven people. Can you do it?"

"I guess so, Ma'am," replied the tired driver.

When they reached Miss Emiline's house, she handed Dan $2. "Ma'am, we drove you to the party, we waited in the rain for you, we drove six of your friends home, AND we saw to it that you got home safely. That will be $27," said Dan.

When they got home, Dan rubbed down Blazet and Dapple very quickly and then fell asleep right in Dapple's stall. Yes, a cab driver and his horses worked hard for their money.

With the $27, Dan bought a new horse for his farm work. He called her Emiline, which was a perfect name for her because she always seemed to act like she thought she was better than the other horses!

Molly Beck, Grade 5
Teacher: Harlan Bultema
Washington Elementary School
Valley City, North Dakota

A Walk Along the Beach

As I take a walk along the beach, I look out to the sea, the magnificent great ocean. I notice ships' sails, bobbing along the waves. The huge, blue and white cresting waves will soon wash along the shoreline and carry in shells, rocks, and debris, which scratch the soles of my feet.

As slowly I walk, I look toward the cloudless, vast sky. Birds fly to and fro, shrieking, singing for joy and freedom. I soak up the sun, bright and radiant, stinging my eyes. As I turn my head from the blinding light of the sun, I see the white sand along the shoreline, soft and gentle to the touch. I carefully pick up a single seashell, smooth and pearly, and place it in my pocket to remember a walk along the beach.

Becky Mason, Grade 8
Teacher: Roseann Bonamico
St. Joseph School
Dover, Ohio

Walk a Little Slower, Father

Walk a little slower, Father,
For I am trying to follow you.
Your many thoughts and actions
Reflect on all the things I do.
Your footsteps are not always there,
And the path's not very clear.
But walk a little slower, Father,
And I will try to be near.
I know you try to be honest
And almost always true.
I don't know how you do it
And I haven't got a clue.
But if you would walk a little slower, Father
And try to show me the way,
Then I could strive to be
As great as you someday.
I know you're often busy
And for me have little time.
But walk a little slower, Father
And *I'll* make sure I'm close behind.
For someday when I'm all grown up
We might wonder where it went.
Our relationship won't be as close
Because of time never spent.
And if I ever have a child
It will want to follow me, too.
So walk a little slower, Father
For both of us are following you.

Marisa Meizlish, Grade 8
Teacher: Joyce Schiff
Bexley Junior High School
Bexley, Ohio

The Midnight Bandit

Lights go down, the battle call;
I make my swift attack.
Suddenly, trash cans bang together,
Footsteps sound, lights flash!

The intruding humans have ruined my feast.
I run back, away from the light,
Into the sheltering trees beyond.
So goes a raccoon's night.

Amy Elizabeth Shoup, Grade 5
Teacher: Timothy Turner
Fairbrook Elementary School
Beavercreek, Ohio

Sweet Scenery

White ice cream mountaintops,
Black chocolate mountain bottoms,
Green gumdrop treetops,
Orange jawbreaker sunset,
Creamy, marshmallowy clouds,
Tan caramel pine needles,
All surround me as I walk.

Brandi Williams, Grade 5
Teacher: Margaret Godfrey
McKenzie Elementary School
Finn Rock, Oregon

The Value Store of Life

What could I buy in a value store? What would it contain? Would I have enough money? As I walked into the store, I looked over my shopping list. The list read: religious faith, family life, friendship, happiness, and financial success.

The first item on my list was religious faith. I strolled down the aisles until I came to it. The price tag read $400. It is very expensive but very important in my life. This value is worth more than money can buy; therefore I am willing to purchase this value at the bargain price of $400, and into my value basket I placed it.

The second item on my list was family life. When I came upon family life, the price tag read ''sale,'' $250. Family life is important and worth far more than the $250 price. I could not pass up this bargain, so I placed it in my value basket along with my religious faith.

As I walked further down the aisle, I came upon friendship. The price for friendship was $175. I thought to myself that friendship was pretty cheap. Many people would die for friendship, it is such a precious value. I looked over all the friendships, picked out one that I felt was very special, and placed it in my value basket along with religious faith and family life.

The next thing on my list was happiness. When I came upon happiness, I searched for a price tag. When I found it, I first could not make out the price, but finally I determined that it was $100, fifty percent off the original price. It was on sale. Some people spend thousands of dollars on happiness, and I only had to pay $100. I wondered how something so valuable could be so cheap. I held happiness very tightly and gently set it in my value basket.

Finally, I was on the last item on my list, which read financial success. This item was easy to find. The price on it read $75. Was this really a bargain? To some people, this item would be very expensive, but to me it is not even worth $75. Ashamed, I put it down into my value basket.

When the clerk rang up all the items, the total came to $1,000. He said that he did not know why people bought values when they could earn them. He asked me in a low voice, ''Isn't that what life is about?'' As I walked out of the store, I felt ashamed. The clerk was right. You do not buy values, you earn them.

Kristen Leffel, Grade 7
Teacher: Carolyn S. Anderson
Sequoyah Middle School
Edmond, Oklahoma

Diggin'

Into my bedroom, don't venture.
My toys are more than askew.
I've found a chipped plastic hammer
And an old gnawed-on gnu.

Most would not believe that
Under my dirty, moldy sheets,
I found some matchbox cars
And some rather disgusting beets.

I caught a glimpse of my homework
With pencil doodles all over,
Although I'd just sworn to the teacher
That it had been eaten by Rover.

I reached under my bunk bed
And pulled out my sister's toy loom;
So Mom says if she ever wants fossils,
She'll just go dig in my room.

Dylan Heckart, Grade 5
Teacher: Patricia S. Ney
Sinking Spring Elementary School
West Lawn, Pennsylvania

As I Sat

As I sat in that room,
I felt the hearts breaking.
As I sat in that room,
I felt my faith shaking.
As I sat in that room,
The walls were quaking.
As I sat in that room,
I realized what a mess they were making.
As I sat in that room,
I was thinking of the things
    the divorce was taking.

Andrea Kitta, Grade 8
Teacher: Christine Novosielski
St. John The Baptist School
Perryopolis, Pennsylvania

Friendship Means

Friendship means sharing,
Love and always caring.
People all united
Without being invited.

It means to be kind
And always keep people in mind.
Soon you are taking part
In a great thing that begins in the heart.

In friendship people don't mind
If you're sick or even blind.
No one could ever replace them,
Those friends who are precious gems.

When we pray to God at night,
We ask him to shine a light
On all the people of the land
Who give each other a helping hand.

Jessica Marinelli, Grade 5
Teacher: Sr. Mary Bertha
Saint Bernadette School
Drexel Hill, Pennsylvania

First Day of School

It was the first day of
Kindergarten for my little child.

She was kicking me and
Screaming and acting rather wild.

She cried. "School is horrible!"
She didn't want to go.

So I told her, "School is fun!"
That I wanted her to know.

"You read and write and talk
And play with all the games and toys."

"I don't want to go to school,"
She cried, "In school there are boys."

"Boys are just like girls and
They aren't mean or cruel."

"Now hurry up and brush your teeth,
You must get off to school."

When I left my daughter at her school,
She was crying and screaming.

Yet, I hurried up and drove back
Home to start my fall cleaning.

At home I began to worry about
Leaving my daughter alone.

I remember how scared she was of boys.
She was scared right down to the bone.

At 11:30 I picked up my daughter and
My worries came to an end.

She looked at me with a big smile
And said, "Guess what, Mom, I have a boyfriend!"

Kristen Ryan, Grade 8
Teacher: Karen Fecteau
Deering Junior High School
West Warwick, Rhode Island

History: A Guide for the Future

Cicero said, "History is the witness that testifies to the passing of time; it illumines reality, vitalizes memory, provides guidance in daily life and brings us tidings of antiquity."

I think these are truly words of wisdom. History is not just the dull past, but a record of time, reality, a guide for the future, and it also awakens our memories. History is not dull, but exciting; not mistakes, but experiences. It is famous people, things, inventions, and battles. People should read more history to learn about the experiences others have had.

History is everywhere—in books, stories, poems, plays, television shows, and even in the movies. Sometimes people see, live, and read history without even knowing it.

History is not a thing of the past, but a guide for the future.

Chau Le, Grade 6
Teacher: Sister Carolyn Bennett
St. Anne School
Rock Hill, South Carolina

Help Save the Earth

Save the Earth.
It's been years since its birth.
We're destroying the hills
Just to get dollar bills.

Rain forests are disappearing
So men can farm in the clearing.
Spray cans are taking their toll,
And the ozone is full of holes.

We're destroying our only planet
With careless ones being the bandits.
I love to live here,
And I hate all of this fear.

I'm afraid of the terrible heat,
And acid rain isn't neat.
The polluted air we can't breathe.
The solution is not just to grieve.

We need to pick up the trash
And recycle it into some cash.
We need to take care of our home,
So listen closely to my poem.

David Copeland, Grade 3
Teacher: Kristi Welch
Rapid Valley Elementary School
Rapid City, South Dakota

The Storm

A streak of light, a surge of power
from L.A. to the Eiffel Tower.

The roar of thunder, the blaze of the rain
gives some people pleasure and others pain

The dance of the lightning, the song of the thunder
makes some people think and others wonder.

The yellow fire burning the sky
makes some people laugh and others cry.

The boom of the thunder shows you its anger
but the flash of the lightning warns you of danger.

The squiggles of light color the sky
forcing you up, grabbing your eye.

The next day the storm has passed
leaving remains of what it outcast.

Broken limbs just lie about
Shh, in the breeze, was that a shout?

It might be my brother flying his kite
but I think it's the storm saying "Good night."

Becca Consacro, Grade 6
Teacher: Holly Martin
Eakin Elementary School
Nashville, Tennessee

The Gray Man

The Gray Man is a ghost that I hope I never see! Every summer when I go to Pawley's Island, South Carolina, my mother tells me the story of the Gray Man as we walk along the beach looking for him. We really don't want to see him, because the legend says that when the Gray Man walks, danger is close at hand. Ever since he appeared in 1882, people who see him know that a hurricane will soon hit, and they know to leave the island.

The Gray Man is the ghost of a man who died in 1882. His girlfriend was preparing for a visit from him. On his way to his girlfriend's house, the Gray Man's servant was attending him. As the men were nearing the girl's house, the servant challenged the man to a race. The young man accepted the challenge and decided to take a short cut. As he came closer to the girl's house, there was a marshy area and his horse stumbled and threw the master into the mud. When he tried to get to his feet, he found himself sinking into the mud. In a matter of seconds, he and his horse were floundering in quicksand. His servant tried to save him, but all of the branches were too short and the man perished.

The dead man's girlfriend grieved for a long time. One day as she was walking along the beach, she saw a gray man. When she got closer to him, she saw that it was her dead boyfriend, but when she ran to him he faded away.

When she told her father this, he took her to a doctor in Charleston, South Carolina, because he thought she was losing her mind. While they were gone, a hurricane hit and killed almost everyone. The girl and her family had been saved by the Gray Man, for if she had not seen him, they would have been on the island and probably would have died.

People have been seeing the Gray Man on Pawley's Island ever since that time. I know that if I ever see him, I will leave the island as fast as I can!

Steve Sibley, Grade 4
Teacher: Dorothy Hallman
Thrasher Elementary School
Signal Mountain, Tennessee

Spirits

Harsh winds blow scary black clouds over the fullness of the moon. A fluffy white ghost scans the top of the tallest pine trees as he floats upward toward the heavens. As he approaches the moon, he sees a witch and grabs her broom.

A tired scarecrow dressed in faded plaid slumps in the middle of the dark field. A snarling dog chases a terrified cat through the rustling corn rows.

Acres of pumpkins lie in zigzag rows in Farmer Bill's pumpkin patch. The pumpkin sisters grin with crooked triangle eyes and jagged smiles on the dusty hay. A skeleton paces to the tune of his rattling bones.

As the clock strikes twelve, the ghostly images slowly and quietly disappear.

Andrea Perry, Grade 5
Teacher: Carole Lynch
R. E. Lee School
Tullahoma, Tennessee

The Journey

My brother and I had lived at home long enough; now it was time for us to go our different ways. Our father assigned us each a different road to traverse.

We immediately began our journeys. My brother's road looked slightly easier, but of course my father would not have picked uneven routes for us to travel. My father is wise; I trust his judgment.

Our father wished us farewell and told us to carry nothing with us. It was time for us to begin our journey. No journey has ever begun until you take the first step.

Across a vast expanse of land, I could see my brother's path, and I knew that he could see mine. Our paths grew further and further apart as we traveled.

My road was very narrow, rocky, dusty, and uneven and contained many potholes. I realized I would have to take this journey very slowly, step by step.

As I glanced at my brother's road, I noticed that it was wide, smoothly paved, and easily traveled. There were many rest areas and amusements along the way. I called out his name, but he was so preoccupied with his own journey, I guess he did not hear me. I realized that my brother's journey was his own and that I had my own to complete.

My feet grew very weary because I had to cross rough terrain. I came to a sign that said, ''Detour, Road Under Construction.'' I did not want to take this detour. The road I was traveling was finally becoming familiar. Why did this have to happen to me? The sky ahead of me looked so dark! A storm was approaching and I was alone and afraid, but I had to travel on. I soon came to a sign that said, ''Caution, Slippery When Wet.'' I realized this road was not slippery with rain, but with tears from those who had traveled the path before me. I suddenly fell, hitting my face upon a jagged rock. Looking up through my tears, dirt, and blood, I saw my journey's end. Standing there was my father. I quickly got up and collapsed in my beloved father's outstretched arms.

He looked at me with an astonished expression and said, ''I gave you the harder road and yet you finished. Your brother never finished his journey.''

My father presented me with many gifts that included hope, self-worth, peace, endurance, and compassion. At the beginning it may have seemed unfair, but now I am thankful for the difficult road I had to bear. No matter what kind of road you have to travel, it is important to finish the journey set before you.

Christy Johnson, Grade 8
Teacher: Emilee Hanshaw
Maude Laird Middle School
Kilgore, Texas

Obsidian

As black as the night,
As heavy as metal,
As wavy as a sea,
As shiny as a mirror,
It looks like the middle of the earth.

Megan Wilmot, Grade 1
Teacher: Joyce M.S.B. Harlow
Bear Creek Elementary School
Houston, Texas

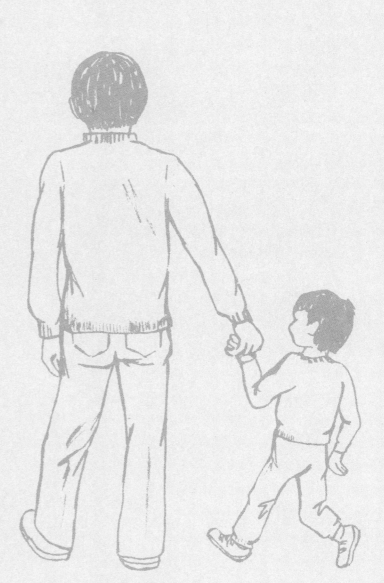

A Lonely Life

I sit here, all day.
No one gives me a thought.
They don't care!
They would just assume I'm not here.
It gets dark, but I can't leave.
"No one will take me!" I yell out.
No, there isn't a soul that cares.
I've no friends.
It is dark now.
Yes, I'm still here.
"Hoot, hoot, hoot," goes an owl.
"Tap, tap, tap," go hooves on soil.
I think of my relatives around the world
As the bright red sun comes up.
They are everywhere.
I've American, Mexican, Asian, European, and
    African families.
People poke at me.
They trample me.
They dig, daggering at me with their giant
    machinery.
Why can't they show respect?
If it weren't for me,
They wouldn't be here.
Life is boring;
However, I am happy.
I get thanks from a pine limb
Or an oak occasionally.
This makes me happy.
I help everyone,
Even the birds.
How I wish I could be one,
Flying freely, shouting at my wish,
"Caw, caw, caw."
This would definitely be a marvelous miracle.
After sitting around for a few million years,
You start to get cramps.
How I long to bear feathery wings like the eagle,
The speed of a leopard,
The smartness of an elephant,
And finally a mouth as big as a great white shark,
For I have thousand of stories to tell.
Or I would even be a basketball.
I'd get plenty of exercise that way.
If only I could jump up and run
6,000,000 miles.
If only I could hear the clocks going
"Tick, tock, tick, tock."
Or if I could tell all of my fabulous stories.
Alas! I cannot, for I am the ground.

Anthony Zuercher, Grade 6
Teacher: Linda Collard
Blanco Middle School
Blanco, Texas

In Search of the Ancient Ones

Can you hear the voice of the Anasazi
In the red rock canyons when the sunlight fades
And the stars fill the sky?

Can you see footprints of the Ancient Ones
In the sand by the stream
In the shade of the willow trees?

Can you taste the dry corn
Ground by hand and stone
Where broken pottery and arrowheads are found?

Can you smell the smoke and ash of burnt juniper
In the ruins of the cliff dwellings
Where the old ones lived and made baskets?

Can you feel the cold wind and hot sun
On the desert mesa where
The Anasazi appeared and disappeared long ago?

Nicole Lindsley, Grade 3
Teacher: Michele Vincent
Peruvian Park Elementary School
Sandy, Utah

Dad's Old Chair

In Dad's old chair I spilled grape juice,
And a couple of buttons have come loose.
The red spot is paint, and the green is grass,
The rip is from when I dropped a glass.
The yellow spot is when Timmie's diaper leaked.
The hole is where I peeked.
Still that chair is the most comfortable chair ever!

Kerstin Karlhuber, Grade 5
Teacher: Joan Wise / Maria Dorion
Sherburne Elementary School
Killington, Vermont

Old Hickory

I slammed the back screen door
And ran along the grassy knolls
Of the field beneath me.
I was running to my favorite hickory tree
That sheds its orange leaves every fall.
I stopped to ponder over my vegetable garden
And I noticed that the shallot was doing well.
When I reached my cradle of nature, I sat beneath
    it
And listened to the constant crinkle of leaves in the
    wind.
I looked above me and I saw the old hickory
Make a path for me with its branches.
I carefully climbed up my sturdy statue and peered
Out of the limbs to see a flock of geese
Parading through the air like gallant soldiers.
The neighboring trees are the gates of my secrets
    and
My secrets are kept safe in my old hickory.

Lara L. Milne, Grade 8
Teacher: Karen Peterson
Ben Franklin Intermediate School
Chantilly, Virginia

Silent Eyes

As I look into my father's eyes,
I see pain like a child's grasp for life.
I see hurt like a flower wilting.
I see the memories of the war—
That Vietnam War,
The place of alarming memories,
As I look into my father's silent eyes.

Felicia Molano, Grade 6
Teacher: Margaret O'Claire
St. Joseph/Marquette Middle School
Yakima, Washington

In the Land of Dairy Queen

Tons of vanilla
and chocolate galore.
Piles of peanuts,
cherries and more.
A river of caramel,
surrounded by brownies.
Hills made from ice cream.
and butterscotch surroundings.
Candy falling down from
strawberry clouds.
This is a dream, I wish
could come true; but if so
I'd weigh one thousand and two.

Audra Szczerbinski, Grade 8
Teacher: Kathleen M. Griffith
Sacred Heart of Mary School
Weirton, West Virginia

Secret of the Magic Potion

One day I was walking home from school and my mom said, "Lauren, I got you something."
I said, "What is it?"
Mom handed me a bottle. "It's a . . ."
"Thanks," I said. I took it to my room. "It looks like glitter mixed in water," I said to myself.
The next day I said to myself, "Maybe it's shampoo . . . We'll see." I unscrewed the lid and a frog popped out! I jumped into the air when I saw that little blue frog with red spots. Before I could land, the frog was gone, but there was a piece of black paper on my bed. I ran to see what it said. "Potion" was on the paper.
"This bottle must be magic potion! I'm going to test it!" I said to myself.
"Here, Buttons!" Buttons, my cat, came running to me. As she stopped, I put a drop of magic potion on her head! Suddenly she disappeared! The frog popped out again. He handed me a note and went back in the bottle. The note said, "You have one hour to get your cat back!"
That means I'll have to put a drop of potion on my head, too! I did it! I entered another world and there was my cat, Buttons. I yelled. Instead of coming to me, she ran the opposite way. Everything here seemed to be the opposite of our world. I'd have to go after her.
I walked into a spooky, dark cave. No sign of life anywhere. Wait! . . . I saw something move . . . It looked like my cat's tail!
I went over and grabbed Buttons, then put a drop of the potion on each of our heads and we were back home again!
Then my mom came in my room and asked, "Where were you all day?" I said, "It's a very long story!"

Lauren Sutton, Grade 3
Teacher: Lois Meadows
Emerson Elementary School
Parkersburg, West Virginia

Ballet Slippers

Light pink in color,
Satin to the touch,
How clear that a dancer
Has danced in them much.
What kind of dancer?
What was her name?
Did these dazzling shoes
Bring her fabulous fame?
Was she a prima donna
Or perhaps just a child?
Did she dance forever
Or just for a while?

Molly Brush, Grade 7
Teacher: Judith K. Schulze
Whitefish Bay Middle School
Whitefish Bay, Wisconsin

From Your Secret Admirer

When you think of special people, who do you think of? John Kennedy? Martin Luther King, Jr.? Neil Armstrong? Well, I think of Yer Thao.

I met Yer in fifth grade, and I thought she was the prettiest person I'd ever seen. She had flawless ivory skin, deep chocolate-brown eyes, and jet black hair—characteristics that most Laotians possess. She was small, almost frail, and had a beautiful smile.

Yer lived in the upstairs of her cousin's house with her mother and five brothers. Yer's father had been killed in a war in Laos before the family came to the United States. She was convinced that the soldiers from the ''other side'' were only after her father because he was the best soldier in the army.

When she first came to America, she spoke no English, so she was held back a year in fifth grade. That's how I met her. I helped her in and out of school, and in return she trusted me. That might not sound like much, but she was so used to being ridiculed by ''my people'' that at first she didn't even like me. When she did trust me, she came right out and said, ''Do not worry, Carla, I trust you.'' It was one of the happiest moments of my life.

Yer and I went through a lot together, but nothing so tragic as what we faced in sixth grade. I remember the day clearly. ''Carla,'' she said, ''I moving December sixteen.'' I can still see the crushed look on her face and hear my breathing stop. When it finally came time for her to leave, I was very mellow. As we walked home together that day, there was no giggling, no discussing schoolwork, only a dead silence. Yer stopped and studied my face when we had to part. ''How do I say goodbye?'' she asked.

''Just say it,'' I replied.

''Goodbye.'' Then she hugged me and walked away without looking back. With my head hung and tears streaming down my face, I trudged slowly home.

Carla Hales, Grade 8
Teacher: Pat Sandlin
Butte des Morts Junior High School
Menasha, Wisconsin

The Energy Rap

Hey everybody! Now listen to me.
This is how your body gets energy.
Your body's a machine just like a furnace.
You need fuel, so it can burn it.
Your food's the fuel I'm talking about.
It gets combusted through a complex route.
Just like most cars and furnaces do,
Your body turns the fuel into CO_2.

Saliva starts to break down the food.
For this to happen, it has to be chewed.
You swallow when the food is small enough,
Then your food moves down your esophagus.
The gastric juice that your stomach releases
Breaks sugars and starches into little pieces.
When the food is turned into a substance called
        chyme,
It moves into the small intestine.

What the small intestine does
Is to get the food ready to enter the blood.
To the starches and sugars enzymes are applied.
Then they become monosaccharides.
When it enters the blood stream, it is soon delivered
To a very large organ that is called the liver.
The liver is an organ that works harder than most.
It turns monosaccharides into glucose.

The blood stream takes the glucose to the cells.
Glucose works as a fuel really well.
In the cell, the mitochondria start
To break the glucose molecule apart.
The enzymes break the chemical bonds.
And energy gets released from then on.
What the carbons and the oxygens do
Is react together to make CO_2.

The hydrogen and oxygen start to get hotter,
Then react together to make a little water.
The end result of these reactions, you see,
Is to release a lot of energy.
The cells will store the energy
As a chemical known as ATP.
The ATP is like an energy capsule.
It is broken down without a hassle.

One more thing, and then that's that.
What your body doesn't use, it stores as fat.
That's how your body gets energy.
From pickles and pretzels to apples and pears,
From bagels and doughnuts to chocolate eclairs,
Your body can burn it to get you upstairs,
Or throw the ol' pigskin or climb up a tree,

That's how your body gets energy.

Josh Price, Grade 6
Teacher: Lois Helming
Coolidge School
Neenah, Wisconsin

Never Ending Sureness

The great grizzly bear
Lifts his mighty head,
The white-tailed deer pricks his
Small ears to the sky
And knows that he is safe in
America.
Chipmunks stop their scurrying and
Storing nuts
And gaze at the dark sky and coming
Snow.
They know they, too, will be safe in
The ground of America.
The bald eagle soars high in the blue
Summer sky
And dives into the fresh, clear mountain
Lakes of America.
The garden snake slithers through
The now darkened grasses of late fall
And knows that he will be nothing
But bones in a few cold months.
But he also knows he will not be
Forgotten in America.
The beautiful great gray wolves'
Lonely howl pierces the crisp cold
Air of November in Alaska.
When the wild mustang of Wyoming
Whinnies into the darkness of the night,
That means I love America.

Jedediah Brown, Grade 4
Teacher: Beverly C. Walker
Sublette County School District #1
Pinedale, Wyoming

The Joke Book
that Could Talk

Once I went to a library. I saw a joke book. I opened the book, and it said, "Knock, knock."

I said, "Who's there?"

The book said, "Mac."

I said, "Mac who?"

The book answered, "Macaroni!"

Holding the book tightly, I ran quietly through the library to find my mom. I found my mom looking at a book about photography. A camera had come out of the book and was taking pictures of everything. As I ran up to my mom, the camera flashed right in my eyes.

My mom and I were excited about our books, and we wondered if all the books in the library were alive. Then I saw arms and legs coming out of the medical books.

We knew we had to get out of the library, but first we had to check out the joke book.

Going by the section of books about mysteries, we ran as fast as we could to the checkout counter. The librarian was going crazy because the books about airplanes were zooming around her head, the books about war were attacking her, and the books about music were singing loudly. The book about Leonardo da Vinci was painting a Mona Lisa on the white wallpaper.

The librarian checked out my book and said, "Enjoy your book! Don't forget to bring it back."

I did enjoy my book and was sad that I had to take it back in just two days. But there are always many, many books to check out, and next time I'm looking for one about space.

J.T. Rose, Grade 3
Teacher: Marianne Penello
The American School
The Netherlands

literacy organizations

The following organizations are among those actively involved in the fight against illiteracy:

Laubach Literacy Action
1320 Jamesville Ave.
P.O. Box 131
Syracuse, NY 13210
(315) 422-9121

Laubach Literacy Action is the largest network of private, nonprofit adult literacy programs in the nation. It uses trained volunteers to tutor adults with limited reading skills. It currently operates about 1,000 local programs in forty-five states; information about these local programs is available by writing the organization's information center. Laubach also operates New Reader's Press, which publishes materials for adults with limited reading.skills.

Literacy Volunteers of America
5795 Widewaters Parkway
Syracuse, NY 13214-1846
(315) 445-8000

This is a national, nonprofit organization whose primary focus is to recruit and train volunteers to serve as tutors of adults with minimal reading skills. It operates 400 programs in forty-one states. The organization can help initiate local programs, offers on-site instructor training, and provides print and audio-visual materials on literacy and English as a second language.

International Reading Association
800 Barksdale Road
P.O. Box 8139
Newark, DE 19714-8139
(302) 731-1600

This association, with more than 93,000 members in ninety countries, is dedicated to improving the quality of reading instruction and promoting literacy worldwide. Most of its members are educators. The group publishes materials on teaching children and illiterate adults to read and makes these materials available to non-members as well. It also publishes brochures for parents about their children's reading. A catalog is available by mail.

Reading Is Fundamental
600 Maryland Ave. SW, Suite 500
Washington, DC 20024
(202) 287-3450

Motivating children to read is the primary goal of this national, nonprofit organization. It administers 4,000 projects in all fifty states, the District of Columbia, and the U.S. territories. With the help of 121,000 volunteers, RIF delivers books to children who might otherwise have limited access to them. The group also has a wide range of publications designed to help parents encourage their children to read.

National Center for Family Literacy
401 S. Fourth Ave., Suite 610
Louisville, KY 40202-3449
(502) 584-1133

The National Center for Family Literacy is a private, nonprofit corporation established for the purpose of expanding efforts to solve the nation's literacy problems through family literacy programs. The center provides free training and technical assistance to program providers, funds selected program models, and disseminates information to literacy providers, federal, state, and local policy-makers, and selected organizations.

Clearinghouse on Adult Education
U.S. Department of Education
Division of Adult Education
Mary E. Switzer Building
400 Maryland Ave. SW
Washington, DC 20202
(202) 732-2396

The clearinghouse offers free information on family literacy. Publications available include fact sheets, descriptions of family literacy programs, and bibliographies.

Even Start Program
Compensatory Education Programs
U.S. Department of Education
400 Maryland Ave. SW, Room 2043
Washington, DC 20202
(202) 401-0740

The family-centered education projects funded under the Even Start Program are designed to help parents become partners in the education of their children and at the same time to provide literacy instruction to the parents. Local school districts in all states are eligible to apply for funds.

Family English Literacy Programs
Office of Bilingual Education and Minority Language Affairs
U.S. Department of Education
400 Maryland Ave. SW, Room 5620
Washington, DC 20202
(202) 732-5722

The programs offer assistance to help adults with limited proficiency in English achieve competence in the English language. They also provide instruction on how parents and family members can facilitate the educational achievement of their children. Organizations eligible for assistance are local school districts, colleges and universities, and private nonprofit groups.

The National Contact Hotline
1-800-228-8813

The hotline is the only toll-free, nationwide literacy information and referral service in the United States. It links people, on a one-by-one basis, with literacy programs in their local communities. The line is staffed seven days a week by operators conversant in both Spanish and English.

they made it possible

America has always been a land of opportunity, not least for its photographers. From windswept prairies to majestic mountains, from colorful deserts to busy cityscapes, America lends itself to the kind of magnificent images presented in *America on My Mind*.

But the photographers, too, deserve credit—for making sure they were in the right place at the right time, for seeing with a discriminating eye, for mastering complex technical skills, and for recording the moments and places of artistic merit for the rest of us to enjoy. They hiked and climbed, watched and waited, shot and edited, and as a result they have preserved the best of America.

America on My Mind would not exist without the creative and technical skills of these 100 men and women. They succeeded in capturing this nation's spirit, heritage, pride, and beauty. For this, we are grateful.

Michael S. Sample
Bill Schneider
Publishers, Falcon Press

Photographers in *America on my Mind*

Sam Abell
Aiuppy Photographs
Bill Bachmann
Noella Ballenger &
   Jalien Tulley
Tom Bean
Annie Griffiths Belt
Matt Bradley
Linda Cauble
David Cavagnaro
Paul E. Clark
Willard Clay
Carr Clifton
Peter Cole
W. Perry Conway
Daniel J. Cox
Scott Cunningham
Larry R. Ditto
John Eastcott &
   Yva Momatuik
John Elk III
Terry Farmer
Bob Firth
Gene Fischer
James R. Fisher
Thomas R. Fletcher
Bill Foley
Jeff Foott
Allen Fredrickson

Ken Gallard
James Kirk Gardner
John Gerlach
Jeff Gnass
Charles Gurche
Ken Hawkins
Kim Heacox
Anne Heimann
Dennis & Maria Henry
Fred Hirschmann
Laura House
Gordon Joffrion
Lee Kaiser
Catherine Karnow
Stephen J. Krasemann
Gary Ladd
Russell Lamb
Wayne Lankinen
Frans Lanting
Robert F. Leahy
Tom & Pat Leeson
Cliff Leight
Ted Levin
Larry Lipske
Thomas D. Mangelsen
Curtis Martin
Steve Mason
Buddy Mays
Rick McIntyre

Douglas Merriam
Mark & Jennifer Miller
Doug Milner
Doug Miner
David Muench
Tom Myers
Scott Nielsen
Frank Oberle
Pat O'Hara
Jack Olson
Rob Outlaw
Harvey Payne
David Perdew
Robert Perron
Larry Pierce
James Randklev
Chris Roberts
Randall K. Roberts
Galen Rowell
Greg L. Ryan &
   Sally A. Beyer
William R. Sallaz
Pete Saloutos
Michael S. Sample
Ron Sanford
J.D. Schwalm
Frank Siteman
Richard Hamilton Smith
Scott T. Smith

Scott Spiker
Allen Dean Steele
Claude Steelman
David Stoecklein
Chase Swift
Steve Terrill
Tom Till
Tom Tracy
Stephen Trimble
Larry Ulrich
Tom J. Ulrich
Don & Pat Valenti
Greg Vaughn
David Lorenz Winston
Art Wolfe

And these photo agencies:
   DRK Photo
   DRS Productions
   Firth Photobank
   Minden Pictures
   National Aeronautics &
      Space Administration
   New England Stock Photo
   Photographic Resources
   Stock South
   Tom Stack & Associates
   Visions from Nature

acknowledgments

The publisher gratefully acknowledges the following sources:

Pages 11 and 56 from *Journey into Summer* by Edwin Way Teale. Copyright 1990; St. Martin's Press, Inc., New York.

Pages 16 and 114 from *America and Americans* by John Steinbeck. Copyright 1968; Bantam Books, Inc., New York.

Page 20 from *The Geographical History of America* by Gertrude Stein. Copyright 1964; Random House, Inc., New York.

Page 31 from *The Necessity of Empty Places* by Paul Gruchow. Copyright 1988; St. Martin's Press, Inc., New York.

Page 36 from *The Mind of the South* by W.J. Cash. Copyright 1941; Alfred A. Knopf, Inc., New York.

Page 40 from *The Sound of Mountain Water* by Wallace Stegner. Copyright 1969; Doubleday & Co., Inc., New York.

Page 44 from *The Edge of the Sea* by Rachel Carson. Copyright 1955; E.M. Hale & Co., Eau Claire, Wisconsin, by arrangement with Houghton Mifflin Co., Boston.

Page 50 from *Collier's* magazine, July 8, 1955.

Page 54 from *Pilgrim at Tinker Creek* by Annie Dillard. Copyright 1988; Harper & Row Publishers, Inc., New York.

Page 64 from *O Pioneers!* by Willa Cather. Copyright 1933; Houghton Mifflin Co., Boston.

Page 71 from *Wandering through Winter* by Edwin Way Teale. Copyright 1990; St. Martin's Press, Inc., New York.

Pages 80 and 150 from *Inside U.S.A.* by John Gunther. Copyright 1951; Harper & Row Publishers, Inc., New York.

Pages 85 and 120 from *A Sand County Almanac* by Aldo Leopold. Copyright 1949; Oxford University Press, Inc., New York.

Page 90 from *The Land of Little Rain* by Mary Austin. Copyright 1988; Penguin Books, Inc., New York.

Page 94 from *Buckaroo* by Kurt Markus. Copyright 1987; Little, Brown & Co., Boston.

Page 98 from *Mark Twain's Letters from Hawaii,* edited by A. Grove Day. Copyright 1975; University Press of Hawaii, Honolulu.

Page 105 from *You Learn by Living* by Eleanor Roosevelt. Copyright 1983; Westminster Press, Louisville, Kentucky.

Page 106 from *Two Cheers for Democracy* by E.M. Forster. Copyright 1972; Edward Arnold, United Kingdom.

Page 110 from *Jet* magazine; Johnson Publishing Co., Inc., Chicago.

Page 112 from *Frontier* by Louis L'Amour. Copyright 1984; Bantam Books, Inc., New York.

Page 122 from *The All American War Game* by James Lawton. Copyright 1984; Blackwell.

Page 123 from *God's Country and Mine* by Jacques Barzun. Copyright 1973; Greenwood Press, Inc., Westport, Connecticut.

Page 131 from *My Antonia* by Willa Cather. Copyright 1977; Houghton Mifflin Co., Boston.

Page 142 from *The Complete Poems of Carl Sandburg.* Copyright 1970; Harcourt Brace Jovanovich, San Diego.

Page 144 from *High, Wide and Lonesome* by Hal Borland. Copyright 1990; University of Arizona Press, Tucson.

Page 146 from *The Points of My Compass* by E.B. White. Copyright 1962; Harper & Row, Publishers, New York.

Page 148 from *The Mysterious Lands* by Ann Zwinger. Copyright 1990; Plume Books, New York.

Page 156 from *An Outdoor Journal* by Jimmy Carter. Copyright 1988; Bantam Books, Inc., New York.

Editing, design, typesetting, and other prepress work by Falcon Press, Helena, Montana. Binding and printing in Korea.

Library of Congress Number: 90-85970

ISBN 1-56044-057-0

AMERICA
on my mind
series

FALCON PRESS®

For extra copies of this book please check with your local bookstore, or write to Falcon Press, P.O. Box 1718, Helena, MT 59624. You may also call toll-free 1-800-582-2665.